REPORT W

CRONER CCH

Croner.CCH Group Limited
145 London Road
Kingston upon Thames
Surrey KT2 6SR
Tel: 020 8547 3333

Published by
Croner.CCH Group Limited
145 London Road
Kingston upon Thames
Surrey KT2 6SR
Tel: 020 8547 3333

First published May 2000

British Library cataloguing in Publication Data. A CIP Catalogue Record for this book is available from the British Library

ISBN 1 85524 562 0

Printed by Creative Print and Design, Wales

AUTHOR

Janet Macdonald

Janet Macdonald's career has encompassed several industries, most recently banking and international finance, where much of her work involved writing reports. Janet is now a full-time freelance writer, and has used her writing skills to produce many books and articles on management techniques.

Contents

CHAPTER 1
DEFINITIONS

Reports are an important part of the management decision-making process. Whether a commercial enterprise, a local or central government agency, or a public body is involved, good decisions cannot be made without careful consideration of all the relevant facts. Although facts can be presented verbally to decision makers, it is usual to present them in a written form which can be considered at length. It is this presentation of facts, which is usually accompanied by recommendations on what should be done, that is known as a report.

TYPES OF REPORTS

Reports can take many forms but fall into two main types: informal and formal. Informal reports are normally those which involve only small budgets or have minor effects on procedures or people. They tend to be quite short and written in informal language by only one person. *Chapter 5: Informal Reports* deals with informal reports in more detail.

Formal reports are usually those which deal with matters of more import and should be written in formal language. They tend to be long, detailed and multi-sectioned. They may also require several people to collaborate in the research and writing. *Chapter 6: Formal Reports* deals with formal reports in more detail.

CONFIDENTIALITY

Reasons for Confidentiality

There are four main reasons for confidentiality, namely:
- commercial competition
- political expediency

- tact
- protection of sources.

Commercial competition
This covers all aspects of business confidentiality, from keeping a new product under wraps until launch day, to guarding against industrial espionage. All businesses must be constantly on their guard against leaks of information which could benefit competitors. Even a report assessing new manufacturing machinery could benefit competitors and while competitors might not be prepared to go as far as actively to seek such information, idle chat in a pub by a photocopier operator could filter through.

Political expediency
This covers aspects from the major, such as tentative plans for closing a factory to the minor, such as the imminent redundancy of an individual.

At both ends of the scale there is scope for damage if the news gets out before any necessary safeguards are organised. The possibility of a factory closure could lead to industrial action, while the redundant individual may have time to wreak spiteful damage before the axe falls.

Tact
This covers such areas as the imminent appointment of a director, who will want to time the news of the change when it is most propitious.

Where senior personnel of publicly quoted companies are concerned, news of departures and arrivals may be designated "price sensitive" and thus "insider information".

Protection of sources
This is often less a matter of restricting circulation than a need to exercise great care in the content. This extends beyond using code names for things which should not be publicly identified, as although unauthorised general readers will not be able to identify coded products, companies or peripheral bodies such as professional firms, careless reference to a date of introduction or a factory location might give the game away to people within the same industry or peripheral profession.

Retaining Confidentiality

In extreme cases, it may be necessary for the writer or a trusted aide to take a typescript to an outside print shop for reproduction and then deliver all the copies to the recipients personally and obtain receipts.

Early drafts, manuscripts, notes and research material will have to be kept locked away until they can be personally shredded. Computer files must be password protected, as should disks, and disks should also be locked up.

While marking reports "For Your Eyes Only" may be a bit extreme, where absolute confidentiality is required, it might be worth tactfully reminding recipients that many people consider the art of reading upside-down to be a necessity of modern business life!

COMMON FEATURES

A report is something which is produced by one person or a group of people so that another person or group of people can make a decision. In their simplest form, reports can be delivered verbally, but they are more usually formal documents which detail facts, reach conclusions about those facts and recommend action.

Although a report can be a method of bringing to a superior's attention a situation which the writer feels needs rectifying, it is usually produced as the result of a request from above. There is little point in producing elaborate documents and detailed contents on a matter which the superior may consider to be of small importance.

In such situations it is preferable to raise the subject in general terms to gauge the response before embarking on a major investigation. A simple memo saying "I believe we may be able to buy photocopier paper at better rates from a different supplier. Would you like me to investigate?" is all that is needed. This puts the report back into the category of something that has been officially requested.

The other main common feature of reports is that they are the result of investigations. It is rare that all the necessary facts can be assembled from the report writer's own experience. Usually it is necessary to gather the facts from various sources and consider their relevance before starting to write.

A good report is one which contains all the information needed to enable the reader to make a good decision. It will not contain incorrect or superfluous information and for this reason it is usual to give details of the source of the information so that it can be checked. The information should be set out in a sequence which allows the reader to follow the logic which leads to the conclusions and recommendations.

Since reports are written to achieve a purpose, and since decision makers like their task to be simplified by reducing the number of options available, all reports end with conclusions and recommendations. Some have both, although this is less common in business reports than accidents reports. Examination of the events prior to the accident will lead to the conclusion of what caused it and recommendations of how to prevent a recurrence follow from this.

Who Writes Reports?

Anyone may be called upon to write a report, but the more formal types are written by line managers or professional specialists. The ability to write good reports is an important skill that improves a writer's career prospects and it is therefore a skill that is worth taking a little trouble to acquire.

SUMMARY

Reports are an important part of the modern decision-making process. They come in many forms, from a single page memo to formal printed and bound documents, but they all have common features. These include an investigation into relevant facts, conclusions drawn from examination of these facts, or recommendations as to what action or decision should follow. Confidentiality may involve rigid security, as breaches could have serious effects.

The ability to produce good reports is a valuable skill.

CHAPTER 2

TERMS OF REFERENCE

If a report is to be effective, it is essential to know what it is meant to achieve. Therefore the report writer's first task is to arrive at a precise definition of its purpose. To do this, it is necessary to define the terms of reference, both within the report itself and within its production, all of which can be done by asking:

- what is the objective of the report?
- what parameters are there to the report?
- what is the scope of the report?
- what authority is available to the report?
- who will read it?
- what is the time-scale?
- what is the budget?
- what resources are available?

The answers to some of these questions may prompt a further series of questions, all of which need answering before the report can be completed. To avoid the unpopularity which comes from intermittent queries, it is best to consider all the areas which need defining and produce a detailed list of questions before approaching those who hold the answers. It is often necessary to admit ignorance and ask the experts what they think is necessary to do the job, but experience with reports in general and the organisation in particular will enable the writer to reduce the number of subordinate questions.

THE OBJECTIVE

The success of the report is dependent on a full answer to the question of the objective. The simple report in *Chapter 9: Sample Reports* — see *Sample Report 1* — was tightly defined: produce a report on staff coverage during the peak holiday months of July and August. The report itself would have been more complex if it had to cover the Christmas/New Year and Easter periods, but otherwise there was little more the report writer could have done without exceeding the terms of reference.

Had the objective been the wider one of seeking ways to retain staff numbers at normal levels during those holiday periods, the writer could have investigated the relative costs of overtime and agency temps, or using school-leavers or work-experience staff during the crucial periods. While all these options would certainly keep staff numbers up, some of them might involve a serious loss in efficiency or additional costs in supervisors.

It is often possible to suggest ways to solve a problem by the simple method of moving it to another area, such as having some of the work done by an outside organisation but has the problem moved in its entirety?

Outsourcing work just to retain full coverage during the holiday period is rather extreme and will bring its own constraints with staff time needed to check the work. It could also lead to difficulties in relationships with staff or unions who might see the idea as the thin end of a wedge leading to complete outsourcing of the work and associated redundancies.

By the time all this has been considered, what could have been dealt with as a one page memo in response to a simple and tightly defined instruction, has grown to a multi-sectioned and probably multi-paged document. It should not take long to think of all the areas that could be investigated and written up. Closely following those thoughts will come the reflection that there is also a one line answer to the question of dealing with missing staff: close the office during holiday periods!

This bald suggestion, although it may be the ultimate solution to the problem, is not likely to endear the writer to higher authority, since it smacks of an inability to recognise the gravity of the task. On the other hand, the opposite extreme of a long rambling report covering all possible aspects in copious and minute detail could be interpreted as an inability to focus on essentials.

At this point it is worth mentioning that the report writer also has an objective. This might include the ulterior motive of demonstrating such personal brilliance that a promotion will follow, but is quite simply to produce a report that helps the person who asked for it to meet his or her objective.

These interlinked objectives are best achieved by eliminating irrelevant distractions. This requires definition of the term "relevant", otherwise known as setting parameters.

PARAMETERS

The first area that must be clarified is the importance of achieving the objective which the report is addressing. Does the objective matter more than anything else? Does it matter more than some things and less than others? Or is it merely something that would be nice to achieve, but is not absolutely essential?

To return to the objective of dealing with office staff absence during peak holiday periods by closing the office down, it is first necessary to define the purpose of the office. Is it essential to the enterprise's survival? This heading covers functions as diverse as compliance monitoring in an investment company or the cashiers in a department store. In the first case, financial legislation demands the presence of compliance staff as a condition of trading. In the second, payments received could wait until the staff return from holiday, but this would soon have a serious effect on cash flow.

If the office is not a legal requirement, is it commercially essential? This category covers all the ramifications of the tasks of accepting and processing orders, producing and handling goods, dealing with returns and other problems.

Clearly, closing down areas that are legally or commercially essential cannot be considered. There are areas where this might be tolerable, such as a complaints department, where personal letters to disgruntled customers could be delayed until staff return. However, if the public image of the company, and therefore its essential loyal customer base, is dependent upon maintaining a rapid response to complaints, such departments join a list of absolute essentials.

In this case, the objective has become more definite: to cope with staff holidays without damaging the company's reputation for service.

Although it does not apply to the simple holiday report example, the next area for definition is the time-scale set for achieving the objective. This month? Next year? In ten years? If the objective is to transfer the whole office function to an outside source, a few weeks allows little more than finding potential outsources; several months permits interdepartmental reorganisation and redundancy programmes and two years should be plenty of time to find an organisation that will not only take on the job, but also employ many of the existing staff to do it, thus reducing the impact of redundancy.

The final areas that require clarification are the actual words used. For instance, a commonly encountered subject of reports, "to reduce office costs" is a very vague term which could easily be wrongly interpreted unless one asks:

- by what percentage should costs be reduced?
- as a percentage of what — last year's costs, this year's budgeted figure or a proportion of income?
- should they be reduced permanently or temporarily; if temporarily, for how long?

When these questions, and any others that come to mind, have been answered, it is possible to produce a precise objective: eg to reduce office costs by 25% over the next five years without damaging the company's reputation for service.

SCOPE

In some ways scope could be considered to be another parameter, but since it indicates levels of magnitude, it should be considered separately. This is particularly important when a problem stems from deep-seated causes rather than exceptional events, for the report may need to apportion blame and suggest preventative measures as well as ways to alleviate the effect.

A desire to reduce office costs implies an admission that they are currently excessive. In a recession, this may be a simple matter of insufficient income to support the expenditure, but in other economic climates it could involve extravagance or lack of control. In other words, someone is failing to do a job properly.

Discovering who that person is and whether the failure is due to lack of guidance, incompetence, or a desire to line pockets with bribes from high-priced suppliers adds another dimension beyond this one, such as a need to introduce a better staff selection system, or overhaul internal audit procedures, all of which would widen the scope of the report.

AUTHORITY

The wider scope of the report, the more essential is the need for good authority for the necessary investigations. Some organisations are rigidly territorial and the holder of each territory will defend it against "intruders". Since the main concern of such people is usually fear that they will be exposed as incompetent or unnecessary, they tend to view attempts to win their co-operation with suspicion. In such situations it may be necessary to be extremely assertive.

This could be done by suggesting that the report will label them obstructionist, but since actually carrying out this threat is a tacit admission of failure by the writer, it is far better to forestall such problems by defining the authorisation at the start.

How this is actually done will depend on the organisation. In some, a simple memo or telephone call saying "I have been asked by the chairman ..." will suffice, while in others it may be necessary for the memo to come direct from the chairman. For the highest-level reports, it may be necessary for authorisation to be given at a minuted board meeting, while in other situations such as some government departments the writer will need a categorised security clearance.

It is essential to have this authority well established before any investigations can begin, particularly when the writer is new to the organisation and most likely to cause offence by treading on what everyone else knows to be super-sensitive toes.

THE READERS

Although not necessarily the first question to be addressed, the readership is one of the most important, as the readership will determine the structure and tone of the report. There may be only one reader, or several, in different layers of importance, namely:

- the principal decision maker
- subsidiary decision makers or decision influencers
- people who do not take part in the decision process but who need information contained in the report
- historians.

The Principal Decision Maker

This tends to be the person who controls expenditure, whether in the writer's organisation or as an outside organisation. This might be a customer or the person who allocates grant funding and since the criteria for making decisions could be diametrically opposed, it is necessary to know quite a lot about the principal decision maker. It is important to ask:

- what does that person already know about the subject of the report?

- what does that person want to know?
- apart from using it to make the decision, what other use will be made of the information?
- does this mean that information should be held back?
- does the decision maker have personal expertise, or will other experts be called in?
- are pure facts required or will educated opinions be accepted or even preferred?
- are there any cultural differences between the writer and the decision maker which the former should be aware of, such as any of the classic areas of misunderstanding of nationality and race, social class, religion or gender?
- are there any other areas of prejudice or enthusiasm of which the writer should be aware?

Subsidiary Decision Makers or Influencers

These might be members of a board of directors or executive committee, or technical experts called in to verify the accuracy and relevance of technical information. All the questions asked about the principal decision maker should also be asked about these people and a few other questions are needed, including to ask:

- do any of them hold views which will cause them vehemently to oppose possible recommendations in the report?
- do any of them have personal or professional prejudices against the report writer?
- will the principal decision maker be irrationally influenced by these people?

People Who Need the Information

The main considerations here are confidentiality of information and the level of information needed. The easiest way of dealing with both is to structure the report with delicate or very detailed information in appendices. The appendices containing confidential information will have restricted access; fully detailed appendices can be offered as "available if required".

Historians

This is a blanket term, used here to cover all the people who might have occasion to refer to the report without being directly affected by its content. They could be archivists, students, journalists or the general public. Obviously not all reports are available to such people, but where they are, the writer may need to consider publicly aired repercussions if the contents and recommendations of the report are controversial. Where access is unlimited and the content highly technical, it might be necessary to provide a glossary of technical terms.

THE TIME-SCALE

This is not the time-scale in which the objectives will be achieved, but the time allotted for the completion of the report itself. Since most reports are required for a specific purpose, it follows that they will be needed at a particular time and it is rare that the delivery date will be left open.

It is essential that the writer should know when completion is required and, if it is possible tactfully to insist on verification of that date, it is wise to do so. There can be few things more irritating than to skimp on details in order to meet a deadline only to find that the intended recipient is on holiday or embroiled in other activities which would leave the report untouched in an in-tray for days.

Obviously the greater the scope of the report and the more complex its structure, the longer it will take to produce. Only experience will enable the writer to assess the time needed for each stage and even an experienced writer knows that an additional margin of time should be added to allow for inevitable delays. This luxury is only available if the writer is allowed to set the completion date. In most cases that date has already been set and the writer must plan how best to use the time available.

There are several steps that apply to all reports, as follows.

1. Deciding what information is needed.
2. Gathering the information.
3. Sorting the information.
4. Deciding on the format.
5. Writing the first draft.
6. Rewriting the final version.
7. Reproduction.
8. Distribution.

Some reports may have to be circulated at the first draft stage for comments which will have to be incorporated in the final version. This final version may have to be approved by a superior before it can be reproduced and distributed.

These various stages constitute a series of mini-deadlines and it is possible to draw up a schedule of dates to meet them. The most easily measured time-scales are those at the end and by starting there and working forward, it should be possible to allocate a specific number of days to each stage, as follows.

1. The report is to be discussed at the board meeting on 21 June.
2. Items for discussion at board meetings must be circulated to board members seven days before the meeting, so the final printed report must be with the managing director's secretary by 13 June.
3. The reprographics department requires three days to print, collate and bind the report, so the approved version must be with them by 10 June.
4. The writer's superior wants two days to read the final draft and may require changes. Allow seven days in all — 3 June.
5. The typist needs two days to make alterations after the first draft has been circulated. Writing the changes takes, say, two days — 1 June.
6. Allow two weeks for comments on the first draft, so distribute it by 18 May.
7. The date is now 4 March, so ten weeks are available to gather and sort the information, chase any missing information, write the first draft and produce any illustrations needed. Allocating four weeks to writing and four weeks to gathering information leaves two weeks for sorting and chasing information.

THE BUDGET

A comparatively simple report, which requires no travelling or extra staff to collect information, no special illustrations and which can be word-processed and printed in-house will not necessarily need an allocated budget. A major report which needs to be completed quickly and printed in full colour with professional photographs will cost more than can be easily absorbed in the writer's normal departmental running costs. If extra costs are involved, the writer will need to produce some costings for approval unless a special budget already exists.

Areas which could involve extra expenditure will include:

- travel and entertainment relating to the collection of information
- purchase of reference material
- fees to researchers, consultants or temporary staff
- fees to photographers or illustrators
- fees for use of copyright material

- the cost of printing, binding and distribution.

WHAT RESOURCES ARE AVAILABLE?

This isssue of resources is related to that of the budget. If a major report has a tight deadline or requires technical expertise greater than the writer's own, it will be necessary to enlist some assistance. It is often possible to borrow this assistance from other departments, thus avoiding the necessity of hiring expensive temporary staff or consultants. The writer should always take the trouble to enquire what skills are already available inside the organisation, having first checked on who has responsibility for the various tasks after the actual writing is complete. These tasks include:

- proofreading
- collating the typescript and illustrations
- production of illustrations
- page numbering
- getting the completed text and other matter to the printers
- producing the distribution list.

SUMMARY

In order to produce a report that achieves its purpose, it is necessary to define the terms of reference. These will include not only a precise definition of the objective and scope of the report, but will also give the writer an insight into the recipients of the report that will allow the structure and tone to be focused for that particular audience. Also included in these terms of reference are the essential pieces of information on the completion date, what help is available and how much can be spent on producing the report, as well as the provision of the necessary authority to get the job done.

CHAPTER 3

COLLECTING AND ORGANISING INFORMATION

The main part of most reports consists of information which needs to be presented in a logical order so that conclusions can be reached. The report writer must begin by gathering appropriate information. This may seem a simple enough task, but if the job is not approached in a disciplined manner, the later goal of bringing the report together in a coherent form will be much more difficult.

STORAGE AND PRELIMINARY ORGANISATION

It may not be possible to decide the final order of the information until it has all been collected, but it is sensible to work out general headings straight away. This will allow each piece of information to be stored as soon as it is collected and will reduce the amount of sorting that has to be done later. It is also essential when using the more rigidly structured type of computer data base.

Storage of Information

There are many methods of recording and storing information, ranging from index cards to computer files. The method used is to some extent a matter of personal taste, but if more than one person is collecting the information there must be an agreement on a common format. Small amounts of information can be kept in a notebook or entered onto index cards, which can be easily sorted into the final order, but where there are copious amounts of information to be sorted and organised, a computerised database will be needed. However, such databases often require a template to be set up in advance, making it all the more important to consider basic headings first. Where this is not possible, a free-form database such as *ask Sam*, which allows headings to be inserted at any point in text, may be better.

Any form of computerised data storage should be backed-up on a regular (ideally daily) basis.

Preliminary Organisation

As well as making the final sorting easier, storing information under preliminary headings makes it easier to keep track of the amount of information that is coming in and to see whether any aspects are upsetting the overall balance.

There is nothing sacrosanct about pieces of information. The mere fact that they have been collected does not mean they have to be used if they do not add anything new to the picture. Unless they have some statistical value, there is a danger of creating an irrelevant bias or, even worse, boring the reader.

Some writers make a list of their preliminary categories and sort them into order by giving each point a number, or by linking connected points with arrows. The problem with this method is that the linking arrows can get tangled, the numbers keep getting changed round and there is a continual need to rewrite the list.

Another method of organising topics and showing where an imbalance calls for further research is to construct a spider diagram (see *Figure 1* opposite).

Also known as spray notes, scatter notes, or brain maps, these diagrams are an excellent way of linking ideas or pieces of information in a free-form way. The problem with a normal linear list is that the first item written down may not be the most important, but it is difficult to remember this when it is at the top of the list.

To construct a spider diagram, a key idea is written in the middle of a blank piece of paper and a ring is drawn round it. Other, connected, ideas are written round the key idea in random order, rings are drawn round them, and each subsidiary idea is joined to the key idea with a line. Further thoughts or facts are connected to the subsidiary ideas by further rings and lines. Each new item that occurs is added in the appropriate place, building up a free-form pattern of thought or facts radiating outwards from the key idea. When nothing more can be added, the diagram is redrawn to provide a more logical progression.

Figure 1: Spider Diagram

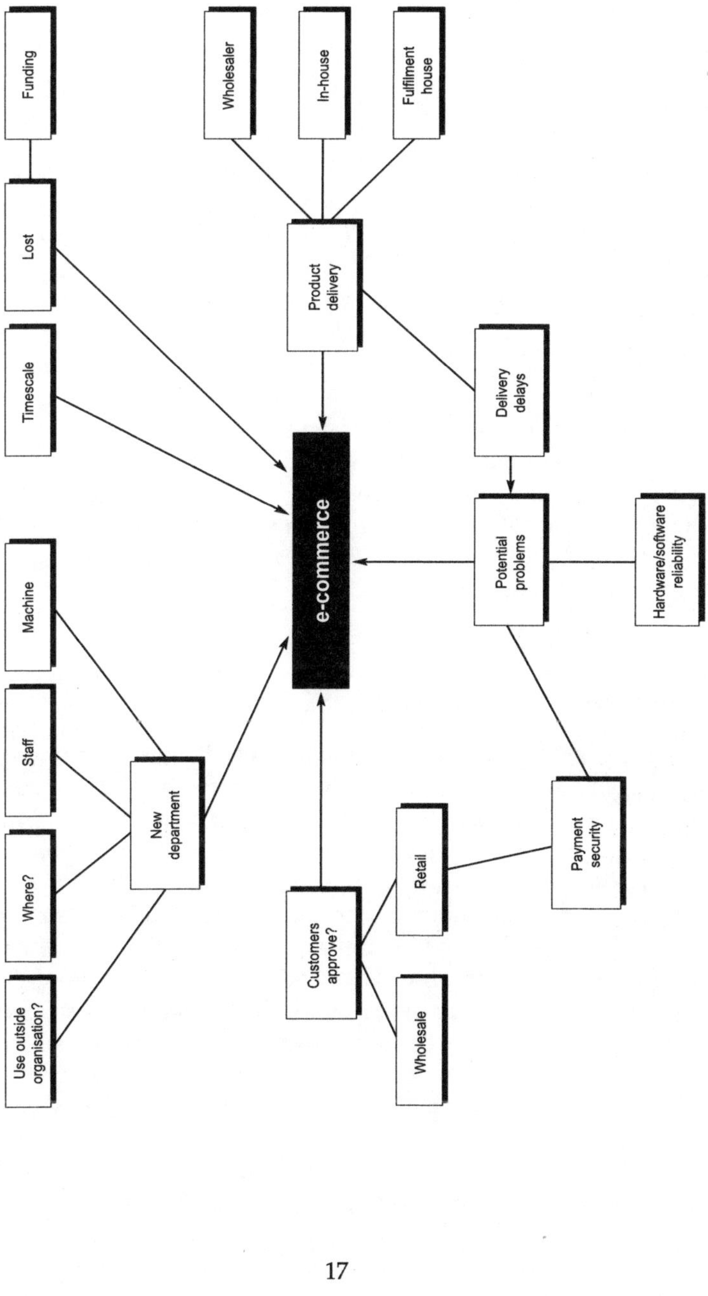

Spider diagrams can seem odd to those who have not used them before, but a little perseverance will prove their value as a way of recording what is known, what still needs to be found out and even where to look for information.

Keeping a Record of Sources

Unless the writer has been selected as an accredited expert in the subject of the report, information will have to be gathered from outside sources. It is essential to keep a record of these sources and in many instances to acknowledge them in the report. There are three reasons for this, as follows.

1. It may be necessary to go back and double-check some facts or opinions. This is particularly relevant to information gained from the Internet, some of which may be mere unsupported opinions from biased people.
2. Giving details of sources lends veracity and authority to the information selected for inclusion in the final draft and allows interested parties to pursue specific aspects if they wish.
3. Where the information comes from an individual or an organisation, it is not only polite to acknowledge it but will also ensure future co-operation if it is needed.

ACKNOWLEDGEMENT OF SOURCES

Where the source is a previously published document, the acknowledgement is usually in the form of references. These are dealt with in more detail in *Chapter 4: Hints for the Less Experienced Writer*, but generally consist of a reference number in the text and full details of the document given as a footnote or in an appendix.

Individuals or organisations are normally listed in a section headed "Acknowledgements" at the beginning. It can be difficult, when there are several, to select the order in which to list them without giving offence to those who are not at the top of the list, so unless a clear order of social or professional precedence exists, it is safest to list them in alphabetical order of surnames. Alternatives include listing them by subject matter or in the same order as the section to which they contributed.

Qualifications of each individual or the basis of their expertise should always be given. There are several ways in which this can be done:

- F.Bloggs FCII, Senior Manager, Pensions Department, Acme Insurance plc
- F.Bloggs, author of *Pensions Planning for Wheel Tappers and Shunters*
- Professor F. Bloggs, Cantab, Head of Insurance Studies, University of Croydon
- Fred Bloggs, Founder and past Chairman of the National Association of Wheeltappers and Shunters.

There should be a clear indication of the nature of the contribution and, in particular, whether it was in the form of fact or opinion. Some useful phrases in this connection are:

- "for the benefit of his opinion on ...
- for allowing quotations from his book ...
- for allowing access to case studies of ...
- for providing statistics on ..."

Where there are several items from the same source, it may be convenient to use a cross-referencing system.

Some contributors may prefer to remain anonymous and this fact should be clearly noted at the head of whatever data storage system is used. Where the report is confidential it may be preferable to disguise the identity of the source by the use of a code name.

It is unforgivable to misspell a source's name.

SOURCES OF INFORMATION

There are many sources of information, all useful in the appropriate context, including:

- the Internet
- libraries
- chambers of commerce and trade associations
- professional associations
- educational facilities
- networking through personal contacts
- professional researchers
- company marketing departments
- credit reference agencies or commercial investigators
- internal reports, returns and other documentation.

The Internet

Searching for information on the Internet requires a certain amount of skill and, where the researcher is inexperienced, a certain amount of lateral thinking. The main difficulty associated with information on the

Internet is that unless what is found is no more than an electronic form of information which also exists in hard copy, it may turn out to be at best biased and at worst deliberately incorrect. Whilst valuable in many ways, the Internet does have a reputation for anarchism.

One source of places to seek information when all others fail is to find a forum and ask the members if they have any suggestions. This usually provides several possibilities, including volunteers to perform the research, but it is wise to ensure that such people will stick to the brief and not go off at tangents.

In the interest of reducing on-line costs, as well as later checking, it is advisable to download Internet material for detailed study off-line, ensuring that the necessary information on the web pages is attached to each piece of information.

As well as general Internet searches using one of the many available search engines, libraries, chambers of commerce, trade associations, professional bodies and educational facilities may, as well as holding information in paper form, refer enquirers to their own websites.

Libraries

Ordinary public libraries hold an enormous diversity of information, although it may be necessary to visit the central branch rather than local branches. There are also many other types of library with varying degrees of specialisation. If approached in an appropriate way, most are extremely helpful and willing to provide information. Some may charge a small fee for photocopying and postage. These libraries can be located through the reference sections of public libraries and may be found at:

- colleges, universities and museums
- industrial training boards
- professional associations
- charitable associations
- commercial associations, especially large companies with training departments
- newspapers and periodicals.

Chambers of Commerce and Trade Associations

As well as having libraries, these organisations usually have a public relations consultant who will be delighted to send information or suggest useful contacts. They rarely charge for this service, but it must be appreciated that the information they provide might be biased.

Professional Associations

These bodies may not be enthusiastic about allowing non-members to have access to their libraries but the secretary or librarian will usually suggest some expert members to give opinions. These members will probably be Fellows and will require a fee.

Educational Facilities

Some facilities restrict their libraries to students, but most are helpful to outsiders, providing it is not exam time. They will have copies of papers relating to the subjects they teach, as well as a comprehensive selection of books on these subjects. The facility's general office will pass enquiries on to the relevant head of department (who will also be preoccupied at exam time).

Networking through Personal Contacts

The writer's contacts will have contacts of their own and some persistent telephoning, together with judicious applications of lunch, will often bring forth the desired information.

Professional Researchers

Professional researchers are available in many fields and can be found through their advertisements in relevant journals. They usually charge for their services on a time-plus-expenses basis, but can be safely left to do the job to an agreed deadline. They will need a precisely defined brief to work to, and will, if desired, provide referees to vouch for their integrity in confidential matters. A cheaper source of research is undergraduates who are filling in time before taking jobs.

Company Marketing Departments

Marketing departments will produce copious quantities of information about their products and will probably continue doing so long after the report is complete and the purchasing decision has been made in another company's favour. The literature they send will, of course, be biased, but may well contain nuggets of information that lead the writer into previously unconsidered areas of research.

If many companies supply similar items or services, a checklist of desired features will allow some preliminary weeding out.

Credit Reference Agencies or Commercial Investigators

Originally used only by credit granters, these information gatherers have become more generally used throughout the commercial world. In the current climate of mergers and business collapses it has become necessary to carry out deep investigations into essential suppliers, potential partners or predators and even senior members of staff. In addition to gathering information on named individuals and organisations, the larger agencies maintain databases of detailed demographic information for most of the world and can split this not only by socio-economic class by postcodes but can even provide such esoteric information as which postcode areas are most likely to buy specific types of goods.

For most purposes, it is best to go to a firm which specialises in specific areas of commerce or industry. They rarely advertise, so can only be located by word of mouth and will neither disclose their own sources of information nor wish to be identified in the report themselves.

If given a wide enough brief, they will often provide the answers to questions which nobody had thought to ask, so it is best to give them as free a hand as time and the budget will allow.

Internal Reports, Returns and Other Documents

Most matters relating to the internal running of any organisation are the subjects of regular reports or returns. Some departments, notably sales or marketing, publish these returns or extracts of them. Since sales people tend to be optimists and prefer looking to the future, it is not always easy to obtain copies of pessimistic or historical returns, but there is usually someone who keeps copies of everything.

Prising such information out of internal audit, management accounts or heads of other departments may require high-level authority.

INTERVIEWING AND OTHER TECHNIQUES

While basic research techniques will provide all the information needed for many reports, there are certain types of report which require fieldwork or technical investigations. Fieldwork can include questionnaires, which have to be carefully worded if the answers are not to produce worthless results, but more usually involves interviews.

The purpose of conducting an interview is to uncover facts and opinions which might not otherwise be forthcoming because the person involved:

- does not think they are relevant
- does not wish to disclose them
- is unable to give written responses as a result of physical incapacity or low literacy skills.

Details Considered to be Irrelevant

This is a situation which requires patience and often more than one interview. Although the golden rule for interviews is to ask "open" questions, the interviewer who believes there may be more to disclose can formulate these questions in such a way that they are finely directed.

Where witnesses have stated that they saw a pile of heavy stationery boxes fall onto an office worker who had bumped into them, it may not occur to them to mention that the worker had slipped on coffee spilled on the floor near the boxes. The question "Do you have any idea why she slipped?" is still open, but should produce quite a detailed answer.

Some of the content of that answer may be subjective. Fashionable young women might say "Oh, the floor was wet, someone had spilled coffee" whereas an older and less fashion conscious person might say "The floor was wet, but she was wearing a stupid pair of shoes with platform soles — it wasn't the first time she'd stumbled."

Whatever the response, it is necessary to persist until a clear picture is obtained.

Unco-operative or Hostile Witnesses

There are three reasons why witnesses may not be prepared to disclose what they know.

1. They feel they might get someone (including themselves) into trouble.
2. They feel the situation might escalate to a court case and do not want to be called to give evidence.
3. They object to the interviewer's manner.

Whatever the motivation, unless the interviewer is in a position to insist on answers to direct questions, it may be impossible to do more than record a suspicion that the witnesses knew more than they would tell.

Witnesses Unable to give Written Responses

These are rarely encountered in the average office environment and in general such interviews are best delegated to skilled interviewers.

Loaded Questions

The purpose of conducting witness interviews is to ascertain the truth, not to put words into witnesses' mouths. There may not be a deliberate attempt to slant the responses, but it still tends to happen. For this reason, loaded questions should be avoided, especially those which the interviewee may interpret as aggressive. The worst example is questions that start "Don't you think ..."

TECHNICAL INVESTIGATIONS

These will include:

- equipment testing
- laboratory experiments
- forensic investigations.

These are normally carried out on a formal basis by outside bodies who will produce their own reports on their findings in a standard format. Some reports will require several types of technical investigation, the results of which will then have to be collated and summarised.

Accident Reports

In addition to statements from the victims of office accidents, it may be necessary to include sketch maps of the area where the accident took place. For serious accidents involving several people, guidance should be sought from the health and safety officials or the insurance company on what is required.

EVALUATION

When sufficient information has been collected, it will be necessary to evaluate its usefulness and accuracy. At this stage the writer should turn again to the stated objective of the report and the terms of reference and measure each item against these crucial factors. Any items that will not serve to further the objective, or that are outside the terms of reference, must be rejected, no matter how dear they are to the writer's heart. Pure objectivity may be difficult to achieve, but there is a dividing line between subjectivity and prejudice which must not be crossed.

It is the readers who must be enlightened or convinced and both the content and the sequence of the pieces of information used must be organised to help them. Whether the sequence is in ascending or descending order of importance, price or chronology, or moves from the general to the particular, before any information is issued in the first draft it must be checked again in case it is misleading, inaccurate or out of date.

SUMMARY

Information for reports should be collected in a disciplined manner, with details of each source so that it can be acknowledged. Information can be obtained by research from various sources and individuals, by interviewing or by technical investigation. Accident reports may also need maps and other details relating to the site, as well as statements from casualties and witnesses. Preliminary organisation and evaluation will show whether or not more information is needed before writing can begin.

CHAPTER 4

HINTS FOR THE LESS EXPERIENCED WRITER

Once all the information for the report has been collected and sorted into a logical sequence it is time to start writing. Even experienced professional writers find this moment daunting, so the newcomer to writing should not assume that feelings of reluctance or even panic are indications of inability to do the job. Anyone who can write a decent business letter should not have any problems with a report, the only differences being a matter of scale and perhaps style.

STYLE AND FORMALITY

Style

To a certain extent style is a matter of readability, but it also encompasses the ability to persuade the reader to share the writer's viewpoint, to transform a collection of dull facts into a rounded picture of an event, a situation or a solution to a problem. In non-business situations, writing style can also allow the writer's personality to be glimpsed by putting words onto paper in the manner in which that writer would utter them, but this may not be appropriate in the world of work.

This is where problems can arise for the novice writer. Since reports tend to be formal documents, they are usually written in more or less formal language. This can lead to a stilted style from writers who are used to less formal types of communication but formality need not be complex. A simple style is the most readable and thus the most satisfactory.

It may be difficult to define good style and even more difficult to lay down rules on how it may be achieved, but one thing is indisputable: good style is easy to read.

Formality and Types of Report

The more serious the subject matter, the more appropriate formality becomes. For instance, there is no room for frivolity in a report on a serious accident, so here the absolute formality of writing in the third person is most appropriate. In situations where jobs are at risk or litigation may follow, care must be taken to use an objective approach and non-judgemental descriptions.

On the other hand, if the subject is not a matter of life or death and the organisation itself is one that does not subscribe to formality, a rigidly formal style of writing can seem pompous.

As well as the type of report, other factors which influence the level of formality required include convention in the organisation and status differences between the writer and the readers. All organisations have their own conventions for reports and although it might be worth discreetly investigating the origins of these, in general it is to conform with those which are long-established.

With regard to status differences between the writer and the readers, a lack of formality in a report written by a junior for the benefit of senior management may be interpreted as impertinent familiarity. The same familiarity in a report written by a superior for the benefit of subordinates may be thought patronising. It is not always easy to achieve the right balance, but there are usually precedents in the form of earlier reports which can be studied.

For more details on informal and formal styles of writing, see *Chapter 5: Informal Reports* and *Chapter 6: Formal Reports*. For examples of reports of varying degrees of formality see *Chapter 9: Sample Reports*.

GRAMMAR AND PUNCTUATION

Grammar

Grammar is a subject that frightens many people, especially now that the general education system pays so little attention to it. Grammar is often defined as "the rules governing the use of language" and it includes the arcane arts of punctuation and spelling as well as use of verbs and sentence construction.

Probably the best way to acquire good grammar is to read the quality daily newspapers; not the ordinary reporting of daily events, but the considered essays of regular columnists whose every word is chosen and placed to convey a precise meaning and effect. For this purpose, the contents of their articles and the opinions they express are irrelevant. What matters is the elegance with which those opinions are expressed. Many of them favour very long, multi-punctuated sentences, but this should not put off the less experienced writer.

Another area of sentence construction that can cause some confusion is the use of two commas to insert something which then makes it look as though the tense is wrong. The rule is that the words between the commas should be seen as an afterthought and should not affect the structure of the basic sentence. If doubt exists, all that is needed is to read the sentence aloud without the matter between the commas.

For example, a simple sentence like "The computer was found on the floor." causes no problems, because there is only one computer involved, and thus it is obvious that the verb must be in the singular form. However when several other items were found on the floor with the computer it may seem that the plural should be used, like this: "The computer, with several disks, were found on the floor." This is incorrect, since the subject of the sentence (ie what the sentence is about) is that single computer, not all the items, so it should read "The computer, with several disks, was found on the floor." "Were" would only be correct if the sentence read "Several items of office equipment, including a computer, were found on the floor" or if, instead of using commas, the sentence read "The computer and several disks were found on the floor."

Punctuation

Perfectly understandable and readable writing need involve no more punctuation than full stops and commas. A comma is used for a short pause, a full stop for a longer pause. In between commas and full stops are colons (:) and semicolons (;). A semicolon gives a slightly longer pause than a comma and a colon is longer again without being as long as a full stop. Both are the cause of confusion and both can be avoided with some judicious rewording.

In very informal writing, sometimes a dash is used to create a pause, or to indicate that what follows is important — like this. In most business situations, it is better to use a colon: like this. Sometimes, two dashes are used — in much the same way as two commas would be used — to put an aside in parenthesis. Another way to do this is to use brackets (like this), but again, they are not appropriate for very formal writing and it is better to restructure the sentence to avoid them.

Sentences and Paragraphs

Reading out loud is a good way to check on the length of a sentence. If one breath does not last to the end of the sentence it is generally because that sentence is too long. Since excessive length is generally caused by cramming in too much information, it should be comparatively easy to break it into two or more sentences by separating the information; overlong sentences, no matter how elegantly punctuated, are difficult to assimilate and slow down the process of reading. That last sentence contained 47 words, which is too many for easy reading. The average reader should not be expected to cope with sentences of more than 30 words.

Short sentences are easier to read and, from the writer's point of view, easier to control; but too many short sentences in succession are monotonous and soon become annoying. The answer is to vary the length of sentences in each paragraph.

This should not be too difficult, as a paragraph should be constructed in more or less the same way as a sentence. Both should deal with just one chunk of information; a small piece in each sentence which establishes the topic, followed by other sentences of varying length which elaborate on that subject.

Changes of topic from one paragraph to the next allow for longer pauses which make the whole document easier to read.

For this reason, paragraphs themselves should not be too long. It is daunting to be faced with a large unbroken block of text and usually unnecessary as most topics, and thus paragraphs, can be divided into subtopics.

READABILITY AND CLARITY

There is a method of measuring the readability of a piece of writing which counts the length of sentences and the complexity of the words themselves. Called the "fog index", it involves:

(a) choosing several samples of 100 words
(b) dividing that number of words by the number of sentences to obtain an average

(c) counting the number of words with three or more syllables (not words starting with capital letters; or with the endings -ed, -es or -ing; or composite words like machine-gun)

(d) adding the answers to (b) and (c) and multiplying by 0.04.

If the answer is less than 10, the writing is easy to read, but if it is greater than 16 it is claimed that it will be readable only by university graduates. Although many organisations will only consider graduates for positions in management, there are still many senior managers who have not been to university and who may, possibly, have quite small working vocabularies.

Whether or not the report writer follows all the complex rules of grammar, there is one cardinal rule that should never be broken: write for the reader. This includes choice of words and length of sentence. It is a basic human failing to assume that everyone will respond in the same way to a given situation, or draw the same conclusions from a given set of facts. Report writers are often guilty of this assumption and fail to explain why certain relationships will lead to a particular conclusion. It is the writer's job to make sure that the reader arrives at the proper conclusion.

One way of doing this is to choose examples from areas known to be of particular interest to the readers. Obviously this is easiest when the report is aimed at a small, known readership, but it should only be attempted if the writer has a detailed knowledge of the subject. It does more harm than good to invent examples relating to the chief decision maker's favourite hobby, for it is all too easy to make some crass error through ignorance.

Tightness

This is a term that puzzles many new writers, but it is an aspect of writing that is closely linked to clarity. Writers who are unsure of themselves, or who have not taken the trouble to check their facts, tend to pepper their statements with qualifying words such as "may", "often", or "sometimes". This is known as loose writing.

It is not always possible to be precise, but it is more important in a report than in other forms of writing. Since reports are dealing essentially with facts, it should not be too difficult to pin down vague measurements of occurrence to specific percentages. It is also a writer's job to say exactly what is meant, not to offer generalities and leave readers to reach their own conclusions. The English language is the most flexible in the world, but it includes many words which have several meanings. Using one of these words inadvertently can make a mockery of what was intended to be a serious statement. For instance, broken down could mean divided, or non-functioning because damaged; single could mean alone or unmarried.

This sort of ambiguity can be avoided by a more careful choice of words or a sentence may require more words. Using enough words to make the meaning clear is not the same as being unnecessarily wordy. Some writers use a lot of padding words such as "absolutely" or "totally" when the words they have been attached to need no such qualification.

"Final" means the last, so adding "absolutely" to it cannot add any emphasis, any more than "quite" can qualify fatal. Fatal means causing death, and death cannot be qualified: if something is not dead, it is alive. Yet both these expressions are so common that they have become clichés. Clichés should be avoided (like the plague?) because they distract the attention of the reader from the content of the writing to the quality of the writing.

Another such distraction is the mixed metaphor, which often comes from the unthinking coupling of clichés. For example:

- "I believe they are trying to sell us a pig in a poke as they are as close as a clam about fuel consumption."
- "They're making a real cat's cradle out of this with their dog-in-the-manger attitude."

OTHER COMMON MISTAKES

There are many common mistakes which also distract the reader's attention. These mistakes fall into the following categories:

- incorrect use of apostrophes
- wrong use of words which sound almost alike
- wrong spelling of words which sound alike
- wrong spelling of other words
- misplaced use of the singular form
- use of oxymorons
- use of words or expressions which are in common usage, but are still incorrect.

Incorrect Use of Apostrophes

There are only two ways in which an apostrophe can be used correctly.

1. To indicate that one or more letters have been left out, as in "it's" as a short form of "it is" or "I've" as a short form of "I have".

2. To indicate possession, as in "Fred's car", which is still a short form of "Fred, his car".

Apostrophes should not be used anywhere else, but often are, incorrectly. For instance, "on it's own" is incorrect, as "it" cannot possess. Apostrophes should not be used with plural words, for instance, "fresh egg's for sale".

Wrong Use of Words that Sound Almost Alike

Here are some of the most common pairs of words which are misused, together with their proper meanings:

affect (make a difference)	effect (the result)
allusion (indirect reference)	illusion (mistaken perception)
alternate (every other one)	alternative (choice)
confirm (verify)	conform (comply with custom)
deprecate (state disapproval)	depreciate (reduce value)
elicit (to draw out)	illicit (unlawful)
eminent (distinguished)	imminent (about to happen)
ensure (make certain)	insure (guard against loss)
militate (to be in conflict)	mitigate (make less severe)
perspective (visual relationships)	prospective (probable future)
rebate (discount)	rebut (argue)

Wrong Spellings of Words that Sound Alike

These fall into two categories:

(a) those which sound alike but mean different things

(b) those which change spelling when they are used for different parts of speech.

Some of those which sound alike but mean different things are as follows.

discreet (prudent or tactful)	discrete (separate or distinct)
de-fuse (to prevent an explosion)	diffuse (widely spread)
formally (in formal manner)	formerly (in the past)
forward (in front)	foreword (preface)
principal (most important)	principle (doctrine)
re-sort (sort again)	resort (holiday place)

Some of those which change spelling when they are used for different parts of speech are as follows.

1. A dependant is a person who is dependent on another.
2. A licensed victualler is a person who has a licence to sell food and drink.
3. To maintain a machine properly, it must have regular maintenance.

Wrong Spelling of Other Words

Some words are incorrectly spelt because they are sloppily pronounced when spoken, such as "Pacific" (an ocean) when what is meant is "specific" (of a particular kind); or "definate" (there is no such word!) instead of "definite".

Words which include both "c" and "s", such as "necessary" or "occasion" confuse many people as to where the double letter should be.

Words which contain "ie" or "ei" also cause confusion. The old chant of "I before E except after C" is only helpful without its second line of "except sometimes!".

In all situations of doubt, the only way to be sure is to consult a dictionary.

Misplaced Use of the Singular Form

Such words which are used only in the plural form, that is with an "s" at the end, are mistakenly used in the singular by dropping the "s". Those most commonly encountered in this form are:

- "len", meaning a single lens as opposed to two or more lenses
- "good", used to mean a single item of merchandise ("good", as any dictionary will confirm, is an adjective only; the noun "goods" refers to single or plural merchandise)
- "bicep", the muscle whose Latin meaning (having two heads of attachment to the body) is only correct with the "s" added: "biceps".

Oxymorons and Other Commonly Used but Incorrect Expressions

Oxymorons are expressions which consist of two or more words which are actually contradictory, such as "new classic", "small crowd" or "working holiday". Other incorrect expressions in common use include the word "decimate" which is used to mean "devastate" or "annihilate" (and has perhaps arisen as a combination of these two words). "Decimate" actually means "reduce by one-tenth", from the Latin "decamare" (take one-tenth). Another example is the illogical "tooth comb" (as in "we went through it with a tooth comb"). This is another example of sloppy speech; all combs have teeth, but what is actually meant is "fine toothed comb", one with the teeth set very closely together.

Jargon and Specialised Vocabularies

Special care must be taken in choosing words when reports on specialised subjects are to be read by a general readership.

For instance, the life assurance industry uses the description "joint life, second death" of a type of policy it sells to married couples for two main reasons: mortgage protection and inheritance tax alleviation. The former is mostly bought by young couples who do not give a thought to mortality, but the latter is sold to many couples in late middle age who can be deeply shocked by the realisation that one of them is going to be widowed. The people who write the brochures are so accustomed to using the term "second death" as a label for this product that it does not occur to them that it is callous.

In situations of this sort it is better to use a different form of words, but where specialised words have to be used they should be explained. If there are many, a glossary should be included. If there are few, each should be explained the first time it is used. If the report has no other material in footnotes and if there are no more than half a dozen such words in the report, explanatory footnotes can be used. Otherwise a brief definition should be given in the text, either in brackets or prefaced by "This term means ..." or "This is the process whereby ..."

The same applies to acronyms. The first time they are used, they should be in brackets after the full title, eg "Kent County Council (KCC)" after which they can be used without further explanation.

CONSISTENCY

Unless a report is quite short, or can be written without breaks, inconsistencies are bound to creep in. Although a sheet of notes can be referred to throughout the writing, this can interrupt the flow, in which case it is better to leave such niceties for the revision stage. Many professional writers firmly believe that it does not matter if the first draft is disjointed, as it will be sorted out later at the revision stage. It should be noted from this that professional writers do not think that they can get away without revising their work! There are several stages to revision, ranging from the simple to the compound:

- grammatical checking
- consistency checking
- repetition and contradiction
- semantics and word choice
- balance
- cross-referencing
- numbering systems

Unless a report is very short, each of these stages should be treated as a separate exercise.

Grammatical Checking

This should never be omitted, no matter how experienced or how grammatically confident the writer may be. The purpose of grammar is to make sense of what is written and what may have seemed sensible after a good lunch or late night, might not do so several days later. When additions are made, it often happens that they disrupt the logic and grammar of a paragraph.

Grammatical checking should be done on a paragraph basis, looking for errors of punctuation, sentence construction and spelling.

Consistency Checking

This should cover the next level up from the grammatical checking of each paragraph, to ensure that nothing changes between paragraphs or even pages. The person used, the tense, the pronouns and even the longer descriptions of people, places or events should not change, eg if an office complex is referred to as "33, High Street" at the beginning of the report, it should not refer to "Widget House" halfway through.

This is most important with names and titles, which must remain in the same form throughout the report. "The Spear Lance and Sword Company" may be abbreviated to "SLS" but should not be called by its full name in some places and "Spears" in others. The same applies to product names, especially where there have been several models with the same name. Spears' "Goliath mark 2" lance may be very much better than the "mark 1" version and those who are only familiar with the inferior version will conclude that the report writer who sings the praises of the "Goliath" lance is a fool.

Where there is any possibility of words having alternative spellings, they must be checked to ensure that only one version has been used.

Checking all these areas is particularly important if more than one writer has contributed to the report and especially if the writers do not come from the same side of the Atlantic. Not only spelling, but many other areas of language usage are different, ranging from frequency of use of prepositions, the placing of hyphens and even some verb forms. (In England, the past tense of "dive" is "dived"; in America it is "dove".)

Repetition and Contradiction

This applies on both the large and small scales.

On the large scale, especially when there have been long pauses between the writing of various sections, it is quite common for arguments or chunks of information to be repeated. Nor is it uncommon for a writer to get so carried away with the details of the opposing viewpoints that the relationship between the two extremes gets missed out. If, as a result of the receipt of late information, the writer's viewpoint or interpretation of the facts has changed, the earlier arguments will have to be amended.

On a smaller scale, checking for repetition consists of searching for and eliminating excessive use of certain words and phrases. Just as the audience listening to a bad speaker will stop listening to the speech and devote their attention to counting the number of times a favourite word is used, overuse of such a word in a report can make the rest of the words fade into insignificance. It is particularly noticeable if more than two successive paragraphs start with the same phrase.

Semantics

Just as those who are uncertain of the spelling of a word should check it in a dictionary, so too should those who are not absolutely certain of the meaning of a word. This is most important when the repetition check has lead to various words being changed for the sake of variety.

This is also the time to weed out the vague words like "recently" instead of "during May"; the loaded words like "alien" instead of "foreign"; the pompous words such as "cogitate" in place of "think" and the padding words like "of all" following "first".

Balance

The sections of the main body of the report should, in general, be of a length relative to their importance. In many cases, over-elaboration can be consigned to an appendix, while large amounts of essential data can be condensed into chunks.

The most important part may have been so boring that it has been skimped on, or an aspect that is of minor importance to the whole may have been over-reported because it is a subject dear to the writer's heart. Either of these imbalances can affect the whole of the report and thus its effectiveness.

Cross-referencing

Whatever system of cross-referencing has been used, it should be checked to make sure that it works by actually looking for the other half of each reference and ensuring that it has its own reference indicator.

Numbering Systems

In an organisation where numbering systems are a matter of convention, this check should involve little more than making sure that paragraph 4b follows 4a and is itself followed by 4c or 5.

Where such things are left to the writer, or where several writers have worked on the report, it its important to check that the notation is both logical and consistent. There are three basic types of numbering systems, namely:

- strict paragraph numbering
- decimal notation or alpha notation
- mixed systems.

Strict paragraph numbering

This is the system used for government reports. Each paragraph has a sequential number, starting with 1 and carrying on to 987 or whatever. The advantage of this system is that any paragraph can be easily identified and located and thus can be discussed at meetings or on the telephone.

The disadvantage is that it gives no indication of the importance of paragraphs or section divisions.

Decimal or alpha notation

This system is simple in its concept, but can become ridiculous if many levels of subdivision are needed.

1. Major headings and sections are given a single Arabic number.

1.1. The first level of subdivision has a single Arabic number after a decimal point.

1.1.1. Each successive subdivision has another decimal point.

(Four subdivisions begins to be cumbersome and any more are risible.)

The alpha version often uses alternative upper- and lower-case letters, thus:

A (a)
A (b)
etc.

Mixed systems

These use a combination of alpha and numeric figures and may use Roman as well as Arabic numerals. With a limited number of subdivisions, this system is the easiest to follow, usually going from upper-case alpha to Arabic numeric then lower-case alpha and finally roman numeric. It is beyond that stage that difficulties set in.

Although possibly the most widely used system, it is the one that calls for the most careful checking for consistency.

SUMMARY

Good style is what makes a piece of writing easy to read. Many reports need to be written in a formal way and care should be taken that formality does not become pomposity.

Good grammar is important and this includes punctuation and sentence construction. Clarity is essential and can be achieved by careful choice of words.

There are many common mistakes which distract the reader's attention from the content of the report. Whenever in doubt, a dictionary should be used. At the completion of the writing stage the work should be carefully revised to eliminate errors and inconsistencies. This is particularly important when several writers have contributed.

CHAPTER 5

INFORMAL REPORTS

TYPES OF INFORMAL REPORTS

Informal reports are generally appropriate in situations where only small amounts of money are involved, or where implementing the recommendations would not have a major effect on the organisation's ongoing management or an individual's career. Such reports would include:

- manually completed regular pro-forma reports
- simple reports in memo form
- other short reports.

Manually Completed Regular Pro-forma Reports

Tasks such as making a monthly return of departmental photocopier use might be done on a form headed "Report". Although care must be taken with such reports, on the whole they do not come within the scope of this book, as their requirements are self-explanatory and they require little data collection or organising.

Simple Reports in Memo Form

In an uncomplicated situation, or one where small amounts of money are involved, a memorandum is often all that is required. As long as the memo does not exceed two pages, the layout can be simple and the writing style informal. Topics for such reports might be obtaining cheaper office supplies, checking on the number of smokers in the office, or investigating the possible locations for a new photocopier. An example of such a report is shown in *Sample Report 1* in *Chapter 9: Sample Reports*.

Other Short Reports

Although it does not necessarily follow that short reports will be informal, or that long reports will be written in formal language, in general informal reports are those which do not require multiple divisions, appendices and all the other sections which are needed to make longer reports more accessible. Topics for this sort of report might be holiday arrangements during the peak summer period, staff reactions to non-smoking policies and provision of smoking rooms in branch offices, or the best time to launch a new product. An example of such a report is shown in *Sample Report 2* in *Chapter 9: Sample Reports.*

Although this should not be taken as an absolute rule, any report which requires more than seven or eight pages is too long to be treated informally.

RESTRICTED CIRCULATION

Another feature of informal reports is that they tend to have restricted circulation. In this context, "restricted" means "not many readers" rather than "selected readers only and not to be seen by others". The whole point of formality is not, as some people think, that it gives due deference to the status of the readers and the importance of the subject matter, but that it can be easily read without misunderstanding by a large readership. Where a report will only be read by a few people, especially where they share a single professional outlook, style and vocabulary, it can be couched in terms which would not necessarily be suitable for those of a different profession. Accountants and lawyers tend to have a very different outlook on life and their work than do software designers or marketing people!

STRUCTURE OF INFORMAL REPORTS

All reports require four basic sections:
- the title, author's name, circulation list and date of completion
- an introduction
- the main body of information
- a conclusion drawn from this information and a recommendation on what action to take.

Informal reports usually require no more than these, whereas formal reports, as will be seen in *Chapter 6: Formal Reports*, often require many more.

Title, Author's Name, Circulation List and Date of Completion

For a simple memo report, all of this, including the date, is taken care of in the usual memo headings: "Re", "From", "To" and "cc" and the date. For slightly longer reports it gives a better impression to introduce just a little formality by having a separate title page with this information on it. All titles should be carefully worded. The English language is so flexible that it is easy to make unintentional jokes or suggest something that is not intended. Such words as "cutting" or "breakdown" are particularly dangerous — "cutting materials in the workshop" could refer to an after-hours dressmaking class instead of a cost-reducing exercise. Intentional jokes are worse. Rather like the twee names fashionable among hairdressers' salons, what seems very witty when first thought of soon becomes cringe-makingly embarrassing. Titles in the form of questions should also be avoided as they tend to beg a sharp answer from the office wag. They are also redolent of the advertisements in the local free newspapers. For an example of a title page, see *Sample Report 2* in *Chapter 9: Sample Reports*.

Introduction

For a simple memo report, all that is needed is a single line, saying something like "As you requested, I have investigated the possible places to site the new photocopier and can now report that there are three options, as follows."

For a slightly longer report, the first page should open with a paragraph or two headed "Introduction" which states when, why, and by whom the report was requested and mentions any parameters or other terms of reference which were specified. This is also a suitable place to acknowledge any assistance from other people or publications which have been consulted.

The Main Contents

In a short memo report, this should follow immediately after the introduction. In a few paragraphs with appropriate headings, it should give as much detail as is essential and should itself be followed immediately by conclusions and recommendations.

In the longer informal report, unless the information is very brief, it is better to summarise the information on the opening page and refer the reader to following pages for the details. This allows conclusions and recommendations to follow straight away, so that all these important items can be encompassed on a single page and thus be quickly available to a busy decision-maker. In formal reports, this brief summary will be in its own section entitled "Executive Summary".

Because the detailed information follows this page, it can be arranged in whatever form is most appropriate. With a report that extends to several pages, it may be worth considering a separate page for each information topic, with a brief list of contents on the first of these. This assumes that there is sufficient material to each sub-topic to make a separate page worthwhile; a sequence of pages which each contain only a few lines looks silly. Informal reports rarely need appendices which are used for very detailed technical information in long or formal reports for a multi-disciplined readership.

Conclusions and Recommendations

In a simple memo report these can be dealt with in a single paragraph, or even in a single sentence: "In view of the above, I conclude that ... and therefore recommend that we..."

For the longer informal report, conclusions and recommendations can either be dealt with under that joint heading or, if more than a few lines are involved, under separate headings. It is always advisable to remind readers of the reasons for the report. In a very short report, ie no more than two pages, this can be done by referring to the introduction, otherwise they should be very briefly restated. The purpose of this is to relieve the reader of having to turn back several pages to read that introduction. One informal way to remind the reader of the objective is known as "givens", ie using the phrase "given that ..." So the conclusions would say something like "Given that the purpose of this report was to ..., and given that the investigation showed that ..., I conclude that ..."

Even in the most informal report, conclusions and recommendations should not be omitted. Their purpose is to present decision-making readers with a ready-made decision. Occasionally they may not agree with either the conclusions or recommendations, but in general the person who carried out the investigation and wrote the report is considered to be the best person to interpret the results and suggest what should be done.

For this reason, conclusions should be definite and unqualified, as should recommendations. Any situation which could lead to conclusions and recommendations with a series of "if" statements should be dealt with by concluding that the investigation has shown a number of imponderables and that therefore no firm recommendations can be made — unless, of course, the recommendation is that a further in-depth investigation should be made and reported on!

Recommendations should be specific and achievable. In most situations where an informal report is appropriate, recommendations will be fairly simple and easily stated. In difficult situations it may be necessary to add tactful phrases such as "high priority should be given", but in general the decision-maker should be able to respond with a simple "I agree with these recommendations. Please go ahead."

OBJECTIVITY

One problem with all types of report which do not have multiple investigators and authors is that the writer can be accused of subjectivity, in both collection and interpretation of information. For this reason any information which does not support the conclusions should not be omitted but briefly mentioned together with the reasons for discounting or ignoring its impact.

Where such a situation exists, it is tempting to write the conclusions and recommendations in a more formal style, in the hope that this will make them look more objective. Unfortunately such changes in style are more likely to be interpreted as an attempt to disguise a distaste for the conclusions and thus reduce the likelihood of the recommendations being accepted. Informal reports should remain informal throughout.

WRITING STYLES FOR INFORMAL REPORTS

There is, unless the organisation is one of great formality, no reason why simple reports in memo form should not be written in the first person: using "I". For example "I have investigated ...", "I have found ...", "I conclude ..." and so on. With more than one person involved in doing any part of the work, that "I" just becomes "we". The rest of the report continues in ordinary everyday language.

In most situations, the same applies to other informal reports, but there may be some situations, such as a main reader who is very senior to the report writer, where the first person is not appropriate. In this situation, although the second and third person can be used ("he", "she" and "they") the writing should still remain active rather than passive. "The cashiers department received the cheques yesterday" is an active statement; "The cheques were received by the cashiers department yesterday" is a passive statement, and, incidentally, a longer statement, as often happens with passive statements. This example is bad enough, but there is worse: "The writer was informed by the cashiers department that the cheques were received yesterday." At this stage, the writing has slipped from informal through formal to very nearly pompous, a style which is inappropriate even in the most formal of reports.

However informal the report, the writing should never be allowed to slip into ungrammatical forms and, unless used in verbatim reported speech, slang should also be avoided, even though certain examples may be in common use in a particular industry.

The point about slang is that it tends to date very quickly and like those jokey titles, what seemed "with it" today becomes "square" tomorrow.

ILLUSTRATIONS

There are many types of illustration available for use in reports. These are dealt with fully in *Chapter 7: Illustrations* and include tables of figures and genealogical tables used to show staff or shareholder structures, graphs, pie and bar charts, flow charts, maps and plans, line drawings or photographs. For informal reports, using one or at most two types of illustration is acceptable, but since the purpose of such reports is that they should be kept simple, neither multiple types of illustration nor multiple illustrations should be used. If these seem necessary, they should be arranged in sections with an index, by which time the report has slipped into the formal category.

The illustrations themselves should also be simple and not overlong. Tables with multiple columns or lines, graphs and charts with multiple sections and the need for "pull-outs" to clarify complex areas should be avoided unless they are absolutely essential to make a specific point and in this case they are best presented as a separate sheet at the back of the report.

PRODUCTION AND DISTRIBUTION

Although informal reports should be comparatively simple, they should be presented in a way that makes them easy to read. This means sections should have clear headings, emphasised by underlining or the use of bold text and they should be separated by a double line space. They do not need elaborate type-faces or to be printed by any other method than the standard computer printer, but for readability it is best to stick to the rule of "black type on white paper".

Nor do they need to be elaborately bound; in most cases a simple staple will suffice and a plastic folder will serve as a cover.

Full details on this topic are given in *Chapter 8: Production and Distribution*.

SUMMARY

Informal reports are appropriate in situations where they will have only a minor impact. They can be in the form of a memo or a separate document, but are normally quite short and are intended for only a few readers. Their structure is also comparatively simple and can be presented in a few sections and in informal language. This could include writing in the first person but language should always be grammatical and avoid the use of slang.

Like all reports, informal reports should include conclusions and recommendations and care should be taken to ensure that these are objective rather than subjective.

Illustrations are a useful way of presenting large amounts of data in a small space. Most appropriate types of illustration for informal reports are graphs, tables and genealogical tables.

Production of informal reports rarely needs to be any more sophisticated than simple word-processing, distributed in hard copy or by e-mail with an accompanying memo.

CHAPTER 6

FORMAL REPORTS

TYPES OF FORMAL REPORTS

Formal reports are those which tend to have a major effect on the situations with which they deal. They may be short, but are often longer and more detailed than informal reports and need multiple sections to deal with all the information they contain. The amount of information required in these long reports may involve several people to collaborate in the research and writing. Types of formal reports include:

- staff appraisal reports
- accident reports
- reports comparing rival products or services
- reports on administrative or manufacturing procedures which need improvement
- reports on the findings of public enquiries.

Appraisal Reports

Staff appraisal reports form part of personnel files and will be consulted when salaries are reviewed or promotions considered. Even one poor report will inevitably have an adverse effect on that individual's career, and a series of consistently poor appraisal reports may even lead to that member of staff being sacked, so the writer must therefore be scrupulous in selecting the terms used and avoid the temptation to use euphemisms or exaggerations.

Accident Reports

Accident reports serve several purposes. They:

- fulfil legal obligations
- provide information for insurance claims
- form part of repair instructions
- apportion responsibility, which may lead to disciplinary action
- suggest remedial action to prevent future recurrences
- provide statistical information.

The forms for accident reports are normally quite elaborate and are often designed so that relevant portions can be sent to different departments. They will have sections for:

- the date, time and place of the accident and, where relevant, weather conditions
- sketch maps of the place where the accident happened
- a description of the actual accident
- statements from the persons involved and any witnesses
- details of damage and injuries
- possibly other specialised areas.

As with appraisal reports, care must be taken when choosing words to describe incidents. There are often so many factors to be considered that careless use of words can lead to unjust decisions. This is the reason why newspaper reports of road accidents use the neutral "was involved in a collision with" rather than "was struck by". It can seem incongruous to say that a pedestrian was "in collision" with a bus, but it would be wrong to suggest that the bus driver was at fault by using the term "run over" when the pedestrian may have stepped off the pavement without looking.

Reports Comparing Rival Products or Suppliers

There are two main reasons for preparing this type of report, namely:

- to aid a purchasing decision
- when the rivals are in competition with the writer's own organisation, to prepare a marketing strategy or product development programme.

To aid a purchasing decision

Where a simple price comparison between identical products is concerned, a short informal report will often suffice. However the more factors that are involved, the less easy it becomes to choose between alternatives. In these situations it is necessary to produce a complex report which discusses the variations in each factor in turn before arriving at conclusions on which is the best buy and these conclusions will need to be in line with any established priorities. It may be necessary to provide detailed technical information, either in the body of the report or in appendices.

Sometimes such reports are required to help a customer decide whether to purchase from the writer's organisation or a rival organisation. When describing the rival's products or services, the words used need to be even more carefully chosen than for the writer's organisation. It is generally considered poor form (and often counter-productive) to decry a competitor's products, but "damning with faint praise", while pointing out the superior qualities of the alternative, is a perfectly acceptable strategy. This consideration can be carried through when selecting technical data or illustrations of the rival's product.

To prepare strategy against rivals

These reports require absolute honesty about any superior aspects of rival products, as well as details of inferior features. They will necessarily involve a high level of technical data, including, if possible, a breakdown of costs. The costs and styles of advertising and marketing must also be considered. Such a report may include sensitive information and thus require restricted circulation. In this situation the compilation of information and the actual writing will have to be carried out in conditions of the strictest confidence.

The writer may need to exercise considerable tact if the report reaches a conclusion that involves scrapping the chairman's pet product. In order, therefore, to avoid career-damaging unpopularity, it is wise to check whether such hazards exist before wording the conclusions and making recommendations.

Reports on Administrative or Manufacturing Procedures

Unless one is reporting on situations which are under one's control, or by invitation from those directly involved, producing such reports is another opportunity to make enemies. Considerable tact and persuasive skills are called for if co-operation is needed to produce worthwhile results. Situations needing such reports could include:

- justifying major expenditure on a new computer system
- altering procedures to comply with legislation
- rationalising staffing levels
- other cost-cutting exercises.

The justification for most of these reports is an opportunity to improve efficiency or reduce costs, but the end product will inevitable involve changing established working practices. Where trade unions are involved, any report that suggests such changes must include details of the union representative's opinions.

Reports on the Findings of Public Enquiries

These are basically accident reports or internal situation reports on a grander scale. The accidents involved will have been major, such as a serious train crash or industrial explosion, while the "internal situation" will relate to the functioning of an aspect of a public body's work, such as the policing of inner-city trouble spots or the teaching of science in junior schools.

The differences of scale are that the investigation of the facts will be by an appointed committee instead of an individual and that the recommendations often involve changes in the law. Where accidents have resulted in multiple deaths or injuries, or major damage to property, the publication of the report may lead to prosecution of the responsible parties as well as claims for compensation.

As may be expected, reports on such serious matters will be presented and written with absolute formality. This does not mean that they have to be pompous or couched in legal terminology which makes them difficult to read. On the contrary, they tend to be models of readability and correct use of the English language, reducing complex situations to terms which a layman can understand and as such are essential reading for any aspiring report writer.

STRUCTURE OF FORMAL REPORTS

Unlike informal reports, which are usually short enough to be read straight through without difficulty, formal reports tend to be long and complex and therefore need to be split up into several sections. Many of the readers will not want to need to read the whole thing, instead preferring to look at the parts which are important to them and perhaps dip into other areas of interest. The best structure is the one that makes it easy for all levels of reader to extract as much or as little as they need.

The full list of possible sections is as follows:

- title page
- list of contents
- acknowledgements

- terms of reference
- executive summary
- introduction
- foreword
- main text
- minority report
- conclusions
- recommendations
- appendices
- references
- bibliography
- glossary
- index
- distribution list.

Some of these sections may have alternative names.

The writer may be at liberty to use whichever of these sections seems appropriate, or may be in an organisation that has a specified format. Where there is not an approved format, the writer may want to create a standard one in the interests of uniformity. This is particularly useful where a report is to be produced on a routine basis, as some aspects may be used for comparison.

Title Page

The title page should create a good impression because it is the first thing the reader sees. To avoid a cluttered look, it should include no more than four items — usually:

- the title and the fact that it is a report
- the name of the writer or writers
- if it is not the final version, the number of the draft
- the date when it was issued.

The title

There is no reason why a title should not be split into a brief main title and a longer, more explanatory subtitle. This is often done with reports compiled by public committees and makes it much easier to identify the report. Whether spoken or written, two or three words are easier to deal with than 20.

Where the title is split, the subtitle can begin "A report on ...". Shorter titles should be followed by the words "A report by ..." Where the title is not a simple, eg "A report on ...", care must be taken that the words used cannot be misinterpreted, as discussed in *Chapter 5: Informal Reports*.

The name of the writer
The writer's name should be prominently displayed immediately after the title, on a separate line. Where there are several writers involved they can be listed on the title page in whatever order the organisation's etiquette requires. However, if there are more than four or five writers, this list is better presented on a separate sheet. Where a committee has prepared a report, the "bye-line" on the title page should state the name of the committee and the members of that committee should be shown on a separate page, starting with the chairman.

The number of the draft
This is only necessary with preliminary versions and is normally shown as the two words "(Number) draft" in a corner of the title page. An alternative position is with brackets immediately after the title.

The date
This should be the date on which the report, whether the final version or an earlier draft, left the writer's hands. Any changes to the content which are made after that date cannot be considered to be the writer's responsibility and for this reason, the writer should ensure that all reports are prominently dated. Dating a report also puts it in its proper place in the historical record.

List of Contents

In its simplest form, the list of contents will consist of as many of the possible sections given above as are applicable. Where the main text is concerned, it will need to be shown under a heading which describes its content, unless it is very long and complex. In this case the headings of the various subsections should be shown.

Reports which include an index will need less detail in the list of contents than those which do not.

Acknowledgements

As discussed in *Chapter 3: Collecting and Organising Information*, help from outside individuals and organisations should be acknowledged, with details of their qualifications to give authority to their contributions. These acknowledgements should be kept on a business-like level, not allowed to degenerate into a page of fulsome thanks to everyone who gave the writer a cup of coffee.

Terms of Reference

Where the terms of reference are straightforward or can be expressed in a short sentence, they can be stated in the subtitle or as part of the introduction rather than as a section on their own. Otherwise they should appear on a separate page, organised into their order of importance and subdivided where necessary. It is useful to write these early on, then use them as a reference when writing the rest of the report.

As a general principle, the main body of the report should be in an order which relates to any stated parameters which form part of the terms of reference.

Executive Summary

Busy decision-makers want to be able to grasp the point of a report without having to wade through the whole thing. They will become impatient if a summary is not provided and may not bother to read the report at all.

The summary should ideally consist of one page and never more than two pages. In a complex report it will consist of a series of brief summaries of the main sections, which should be written after those sections are compiled, not before. Doing this often shows up any faults in the logic or areas that need more detail and it eliminates the danger of tailoring the report to the summary rather than the other way round.

In its simplest form the summary needs no more than three paragraphs, as follows.

1. A brief statement of the purpose of the report and the terms of reference. In a scientific report, a mention of any relevant limitations may be included.
2. A summary of the main body of the report, broken up into sentences that can be linked to the headings used in the report itself.

3. A final paragraph covering the conclusions and recommendations. Although this paragraph should not be too wordy, it must be sufficiently detailed for the readers to follow the logic that has lead to the conclusions.

Where a more complex report is involved, the summary can be extended by adding more paragraphs about the main body, or dealing with the conclusions and recommendations separately.

The best way to write a summary is to ignore the "two pages only" restriction and write as long a summary, within reason, as seems necessary to cover all the material. Then go through it and weed out anything which is not essential to understanding. It is always easier to cut out excess material than to add essentials later.

The final step is to apply the technique used by journalists working to a wordage limit. This involves examining each sentence to see if any individual words can be omitted or phrases reworded to shorten them. "We believe that" becomes "we think", or "we are now in a position to unveil" becomes "we can show".

When deciding what can be cut out or reworded, it is important to remember that the summary should stand on its own. In many instances it will be circulated without the rest of the report, often to senior people who have no particular interest in the subject but who feel that they should be kept informed. It is these people who tend to get hold of the wrong end of the stick, so the summary must be as balanced as the rest of the report and should not omit anything which is essential to the logic of the conclusions. If any of the proposals call for urgent action, this fact must be clearly shown in the summary as well as in the recommendations section.

Since it should stand on its own, the summary must bear the title of the report, any relevant reference codes, an indication of its confidentiality and the date and the writer's name.

Introduction

The purpose of an introduction is to describe why the report was commissioned. If this is covered in the title or subtitle, there is no need for an introduction. However, the background to a situation which gives rise to a report is generally more complex than can be dealt with in a single sentence. An alternative is a brief description of the terms of reference if these have not been stated separately.

It may be appropriate to give some details of how information was gathered and what limitations, if any, were imposed. Again, a brief mention is all that is needed rather than a full statement of the parameters.

Foreword

Forewords tend to be written by someone other than the writer of the main text. This is usually someone in a senior position who feels they should be represented and although the writer will not be able to omit such a foreword, it may be necessary to apply some subtle editing to tone down irrelevancies or pomposity.

Where the writer is in a junior position and the recommendations are for radical action, it might be helpful to get someone more senior to provide a foreword, thus adding authority to the report.

Main Text

This is the most important part of the report and it should be organised so that it is both inviting and easy to read. It should fall naturally into main themes and supporting sub-themes, arranged in a pattern that leads to logical conclusions and it should be clear from the heading chosen for each theme what is to be found in the text. As with title of the report, words that have alternative meanings should be avoided.

Where a great deal of disparate information has been gathered, or where a technical or laboratory process is involved, there may need to be a separate section headed "Procedures" or "Methods and Materials". This section would be followed by another with detailed test results and yet another to discuss those results and their implications. Even a non-technical report might need a discussion of the writer's own results when considered against other similar studies. Some of this detail could be presented as appendices.

All these headings should be shown in the list of contents.

Minority Reports

Where a report has been written by a committee, or as a result of a committee's enquiries, there may be some members who disagree with the majority opinion. In this case a minority report must be included, immediately after the rest of the main text.

It should be clearly shown in the list of contents and mentioned in any introduction or foreword. It could be the reason for the foreword, but in this case reference should only be in the form of a statement that unanimous agreement could not be reached and thus a minority report has been included.

It should be written under the same terms of reference and within the same parameters as the rest of the report. It should not contain any criticism of the majority opinion nor of those who hold that opinion.

Unless the names of those who hold the minority opinion have been mentioned in the foreword, they should be shown at the beginning of the minority report.

The need for a minority report could arise for various reasons, such as:

- a difference in political outlook, resulting in objections to the conclusions or recommendations
- a difference of opinion over the interpretation of the test results
- a feeling that the investigation did not uncover all the relevant facts.

Conclusions and Recommendations

Most senior managers and other decision-makers want to be presented with a simple decision: do we do it or don't we? The "it" usually refers to a firm recommendation from someone who has weighed all the facts before making the proposal. Obviously, if a large sum of money is involved, the facts may be double checked by an expert, but in general the person who carried out the investigation and wrote the report is considered to be the best person to draw conclusions and make recommendations.

Conclusions

The conclusions should start by stating the purpose of the report. This is not needless repetition but a necessary reminder to the reader who will otherwise have to flip back to the beginning of the report to check.

Where the purpose of the report is simple it need only be stated briefly at the beginning of this section, but where the purpose is complex, it may be necessary to restate each part as a preamble to that part of the conclusions. This can be done by setting the whole purpose out as a series of numbered parts and then using the same numbering system to set out the conclusions, or by referring to each part of the purpose as a "given" — see the discussion on this technique in *Conclusions and Recommendations* in *Chapter 5: Informal Reports* (page 44).

Numbering the parts is the most appropriate method where the whole of the report is presented in this format. If possible, the numbers used should correspond with the relevant part of the main body of the report. If not, it is advisable to use a different numbering system, as otherwise the reader can become confused at point 2(a) in the conclusions referring to 3(a) in the main body.

It is likely that the evidence will not only be in one section, but scattered throughout the main body. By the very nature of reports, the findings are unlikely to occur in a simple linear fashion and where this happens the conclusions should be carefully cross-referenced.

The evidence used to arrive at the conclusions should all be in the main body. If it is not, it must be added at the appropriate point, not introduced for the first time in this section. Conclusions can only be drawn after all the evidence has been examined.

The conclusions themselves should not be qualified in any way. If it seems necessary that they should, it can only be because insufficient information was found to indicate a definite conclusion. It may be that the situation is one where only time will provide sufficient evidence for a firm conclusion, in which case all that can be done is to state that the investigation proved inconclusive and recommend that further research should be undertaken.

Conclusions are sometimes known as findings.

Recommendations

Recommendations naturally follow from conclusions and they should not be omitted. Even if the conclusion drawn is that nothing is wrong, it should be recommended that no action should be taken.

Recommendations may be put in a separate section or added to the end of the conclusions under a joint heading. This is most appropriate when the recommendations are simple, for instance that one particular make of car should be bought, or that head office should be moved to a particular location.

However, where there are multiple recommendations, they should be listed under their own heading. In some types of reports, eg those following public enquiries, recommendations are made throughout the report; the word "recommended" is emphasised by underlining or italic print throughout the report and all recommendations are then repeated in a "Summary of Findings and Recommendations". Where this is done, they should still be summarised separately.

Like conclusions, recommendations should be unqualified. This section is no place for a sequence of "if" statements. They should be achievable, and, for this reason as well as political tact, it may be necessary to recommend that "efforts should be made" or "a high priority should be given".

Such woolly statements are only possible when no dire consequences will result from failure to act. Where legal requirements, or considerations of safety are concerned, recommendations must be for specific action to be carried out by a specified time. As a general principle, recommendations should include a time-scale for completion.

Multiple recommendations should be listed in order of importance and each segment should include a completion date. It is perfectly reasonable to make one sweeping recommendation, such as "Head Office should be moved to Melton Mowbray, with the move completed by November 2003" and then continue "In order to achieve this, it will be necessary to do the following.

1. Appoint architects by 31 March 2001.
2. Appoint builders by 30 June 2001.
3. Brief Public Relations agency by 31 December 2002.
4. Draw up staff relocation, redundancy and recruitment plans for operation commencing by 31 March 2003.
5. Appoint and brief removal firm by 31 May 2003.
6. Finalise details for opening ceremony by 31 August 2003."

Wherever possible and tactful, the writer should state not only what should be done and when it should be completed, but indicate who should do it. Those chosen may not be the most obvious choices and where this applies, the reasons should be given. These reasons should not be over-elaborated: suggestions for departure from tradition will inevitably lead to discussions and the writer should keep something in reserve for this time.

The writer should never forget the possibility of being called to meetings to justify or elaborate on the recommendations. These may be from an outsider, such as the local fire officer, but in general it is the writer who has the responsibility for stating "I recommend".

This is one of the principal reasons for signing a report: that signature is an acceptance of responsibility. In some organisations it is the practice for the report writer's superior to sign the report as well, thus adding a higher level of responsibility as well as approval.

Appendices

Also known as attachments, annexes or exhibits, appendices allow the writer to cater for all levels of reader. Most readers will be happy enough to accept the writer's précis of technical data or other detailed information, but specialists and pedants will want to see the details in full.

The best place for these details is in a separate area where they will not interfere with the main flow of the report. If there are different tranches of detailed information, they should be separated into subject headings of their own and each shown as a different appendix.

Appendices can be used for statistics, detailed results of technical tests, copies of contracts and many other items. They should not be used for graphs, charts or maps which need to be referred to when reading the main text, unless they are physically bound into the report in such a way that they can be unfolded to be visible alongside the text. This can be useful when the same item is referred to in several different places.

Appendices can be referred to in the text in a number of ways, for example:

- "(see Appendix A)"
- "detailed results are shown in Appendix B"
- "the conditions under which these opacities build up are described in Appendix C".

Appendices can be designated by letters or by numbers, or, when they have to be sub-divided, by a combination: eg A1, A2, A3. Although the usual sequence is A, B, C, D and so on, occasionally they will be designated by the capital letter of the main heading where they are mentioned.

Under this system, a report with the three sections "Convention Qualification", "Managers' Bonuses" and "Production Targets" would have appendices C, M and P. This system is rather confusing and should be avoided unless it is an approved organisational practice, especially when there are two unconnected headings beginning with the same letter and they have to be designated M1 and M2.

References

This is a list of all books, papers or unpublished work such as letters, which have been specifically referred to or quoted from in the text. It is presented in the order in which the items were referred to, with each entry number and the date on which that edition was published, followed by the name of the publishers. If it is an article in a journal or periodical, the title of the article and the author should be given, followed by the title of the journal, the volume number, issue number and page number. If it is an unpublished paper or letter, the title of the paper and the date when it was written or the date of the letter and an indication of the addressee should be given.

As soon as it becomes apparent that references will be needed, the writer should record the necessary details so that they can be slotted into place during writing and also make a note of whether permission has been granted for quotations. It is the writer's responsibility to obtain these permissions. Failure to do so may be an infringement of copyright.

There are various ways of showing references in the text. Where there are only a few, asterisks can be used with footnotes giving the details, and the list can be omitted. Otherwise numbers are used, either surmounting the text, thus: 2, but sometimes in square brackets after the word, thus: [2].

Bibliography

This is a list of published items which have not been referred to in the text, but which have proved valuable to the writer and will enlighten the reader. It is sometimes headed "Further Reading" instead of "Bibliography".

The items in a bibliography are listed in alphabetical order of the author's surname and should give the same details as in a reference list, so that copies can be found in a library or bookshop. When there is a list of references and a bibliography, it is customary to list the references first.

Glossary

A glossary becomes necessary when a technical report, which of necessity uses technical terms, will be read by the general public or members of staff such as accountants, whose own area of expertise does not require a technical vocabulary. It is also useful where verbatim witness statements have used localised slang, or where a word has a different meaning in a technical context from that in the everyday world, eg "strangeness" as a property of particles in nuclear physics.

Index

It should not be necessary to have an index unless the report is very long and complex with much cross-referencing between various sections and appendices. In general, the organisation of the main body of the report should avoid these cross-references and sufficient subheadings listed in the table of contents should render an index unnecessary. Where an index is needed, it should be prepared by the writer, who is the best judge of whether items should be included.

Distribution List

Some report writers favour putting the distribution list on the title page. Provided the list contains no more than six names or designations such as "directors and senior managers" this is tolerable. More than six names will clutter up the title page unacceptably and thus should be listed on a separate sheet of paper bound into the report, or on a separate memo.

Footnotes

Footnotes distract the reader. In a short report, where a glossary or reference list containing only two or three items would look silly, they may be unavoidable. In general, rephrasing usually renders them unnecessary.

WRITING STYLES FOR FORMAL REPORTS

The best way to think of formal writing is that it is like writing a letter to a stranger. It should not be too chatty, for fear of being thought over-familiar, but on the other hand it should not fall into pomposity and the passive mode.

In general, formality tends to be more wordy than informality. "We think ..." is informal, "This department thinks ..." is fairly formal, while "It is the belief of the department that ..." borders on the pompous. Note that each of these styles removes itself further and further from the actual writer.

Pomposity is often a result of the desire to impress by using important sounding words. Typical examples will have several syllables instead of one or two, such as "modifications" instead of "changes", "remuneration package" instead of "salary", or "utilise" instead of "use". These words may be tolerable in a very formal context, but are merely ludicrous when describing everyday events.

Formal writing does not necessarily have to be in the third person, but inexperienced writers often resort to this form in the mistaken belief that it is easier to write. It can be, but there is a pitfall here for the unwary, in that it can become convoluted and extremely tiresome to read.

Formal reports should, however, always be grammatically correct and should avoid slang, unless reporting the words as part of a witness statement.

ILLUSTRATIONS

As most formal reports are quite long, they are able to support more illustrations than informal reports, although they should never be used unless really necessary. In general, long tables and multiple sets of graphs or other figures are best put in an appendix at the back, with a reference in the text directing the reader to them. *Chapter 7: Illustrations* gives full details of all the types of illustration available.

PRODUCTION AND DISTRIBUTION

The more important the topic of a formal report and the more material it contains, the more thought needs to be given to its layout and printing. Each section should start on a new page, there should be a list of contents and perhaps even an index.

The printing and binding should also be commensurate with the importance of the contents. In some cases the report may merit full letter-press printing with colour photographs; in others in-house printing and binding will be acceptable. It never does any harm to divide sections with tabbed cards or at least single sheets of coloured paper to mark the divisions.

However copies of the report are physically delivered, each one should always be accompanied by a letter or formal memo stating that the report is enclosed. For confidential reports, the recipients should be asked to acknowledge receipt.

SUMMARY

All reports need a structure which makes it easy for readers to extract what they need. Formal reports tend to be long and complex and therefore need numerous sections and appendices, together with a list of contents to show what the sections contain. Some organisations lay down the format for their reports but in most cases it is left to the writer to decide what is most suitable.

A brief executive summary should be written, which should be capable of standing on its own. Reports should finish with conclusions and recommendations, either together in one section or separately in two sections. These sections should commence with a restatement of the purpose of the report. Conclusions and recommendations should be unqualified and both should be related to the relevant portions of the main report.

The writer must be prepared to accept responsibility for the recommendations by signing the report.

Formal reports need not necessarily be written in ultra-formal language, but should always be grammatically correct and avoid the use of slang or over-familiar terms.

Formal reports can support many types of illustration, but large numbers of illustrations are better placed in appendices rather than in the body of the report.

CHAPTER 7

ILLUSTRATIONS

TYPES OF ILLUSTRATIONS

Words are not the ideal tool to convey some types of information. Of course, if enough words are used, the message can be conveyed, but only in a way that wastes time and space and is frequently confusing to the reader. In such cases, it is better to use one of the many available forms of illustration.

Numerical or Statistical Data

Sometimes, when sets of numbers are involved, they can be rendered accessible by rewriting in prose form, by presenting the sentence so that each figure starts a phrase on a new line, as follows:

Instead of writing "This month, 361 widgets per day were made by 23 machinists, which averages out at 16 each" the information can be written like this:

"This month,

23 machinists produced
361 widgets per day, or an average of
16 widgets each."

Even this simple example of three sets of figures is easier to read when it is set out vertically instead of horizontally. Multiply the situation by adding more months and even this vertical version would become much more difficult to follow. It is at this point that words need to give way to illustrations or diagrams. In the case of widget production, a table such as that shown in *Figure 6b* later in this chapter (on page 73) could be used.

Illustrations for numerical data can take many forms, some of which are interchangeable. Whatever type of illustration is chosen, they should only be used when they make the point more effectively than words. Care should be taken that they do not themselves confuse, as can happen when too much information is crammed into one diagram, rather than spread among several.

More confusion can be caused by illustrations that have been produced without sufficient thought being given to the component parts. There are many optical illusions of simple figures which are well known to graphic artists, but which might not occur to a non-artistic report writer who assumes that there is no need to pay an artist for what seems merely straight lines, circles or squares.

The problem with many optical illusions is that what is perceived by one person at first glance is often different from what is perceived by another. A blink or slight movement of the page usually shows the alternative picture, but some people are never able to see it.

Figure 2 and *Figure 3* show two classic examples of this phenomenon: the ornate goblet that transforms into two people face to face and the series of cross-hatched lines which might be parallel or might taper.

Figure 2: Ornate Goblet Optical Illusion

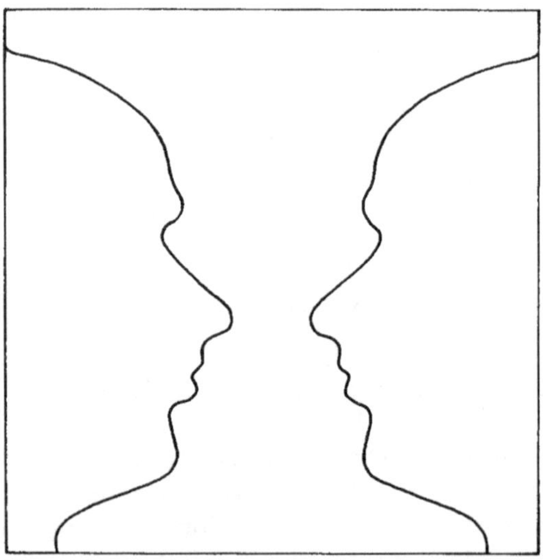

Figure 3: Parallel or Tapering Lines Optical Illusion

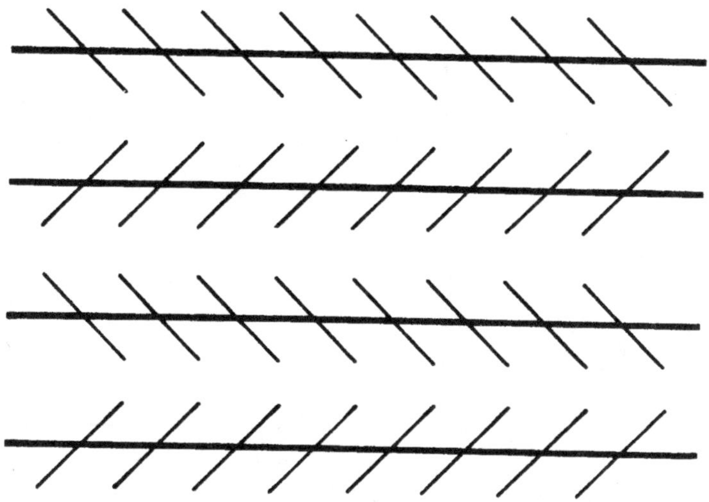

A further sequence of problems comes with pictures which are intended to show comparisons, but fail to do so because of the differences in perception of light and dark shades, or of perspective. *Figure 4* and *Figure 5* overleaf show examples of these.

As a general rule it is safer to use graphs or bar charts for comparisons, as most people find it easier to compare two straight lines than two circles, squares or other geometrical figures. This is why the type of illustration chosen for any given purpose has often become a matter of convention. Where such a convention exists it is wisest to stick to it as most readers prefer to be given information in a familiar form. The most common methods of showing numerical or statistical data are:

- tables
- graphs
- bar charts
- pie charts
- pictograms.

Tables

Tables consist of columns of figures. Each column is topped by a heading which identifies the figures below. Whenever space permits, these headings should be shown horizontally so that they can be read without having to turn the table round. When space is scarce, the

Figure 4: Effect of Perspective (1)

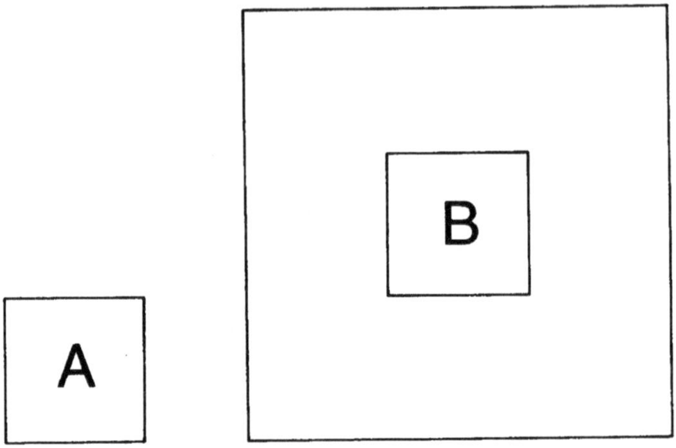

Figure 5: Effect of Perspective (2)

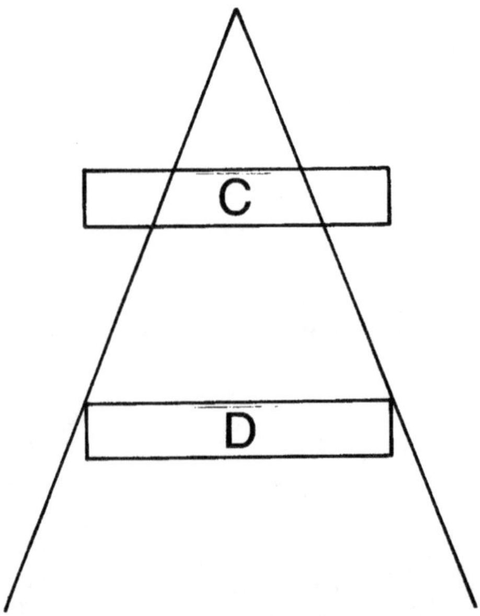

headings should be on a clockwise slant, rather than shown by placing the letters from top to bottom (see *Figure 6a* below).

Figure 6a: Table (1)

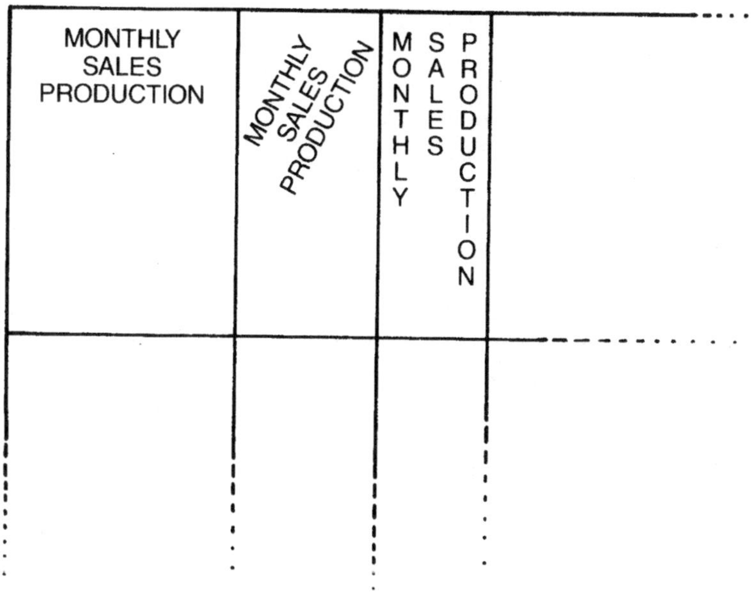

Opinions differ on whether headings should be centred in the column or aligned to the left.

Headings should be at the very top of each column, followed by an indication of the status of the figures below. Money is shown by the sterling (£) sign, with pence indicated by use of a decimal point rather than actually being shown in the heading. Rounding of large figures is shown by an "x" and a sequence of zeros to indicate the magnitude. Zero means "power of 10", so "x000" means the figures in the column are thousands. These are sometimes indicated by using "K" for thousands and "M" for millions (not "m", which is universally accepted as meaning metres).

Rounding is generally accepted in tables relating to money, but the magnitude of the rounding is dependent on the subject matter. International conglomerates will round the figures in their annual reports to one decimal point of millions, eg $6.7, whereas an internal report comparing the price of widgets will only round up to pounds. The grommet pins for the widgets which cost pennies each, will be shown as £0.07.

Other tables, particularly those relating to scientific, chemical or engineering data which need to be precise will show figures to several decimal points.

Tables are easier to follow if they are presented in small blocks. As long as there is adequate space between each column of figures, they do not necessarily have to be divided by vertical lines, but it does make for easier reading to add some vertical lines, say at intervals of no more than six columns. This makes it easier to scan down a column without the eye slipping to the wrong column. Horizontal lines are usually reserved for isolating headings and totals, but spaces every few lines are helpful in long columns. If there is no natural division of data, leaving a space after every three lines breaks the figures up into acceptable chunks. *Figure 6b* opposite shows a simple table.

Graphs

Graphs are used either to show trends or the relationships between two or more related factors. Examples of the first type can be seen regularly in the business sections of newspapers, showing the progression of inflation or stock market prices. The latter can be found in books on economic history, showing the relationship between mortgage rates, stamp duty on house purchases and the prices of houses.

Graphs are easier to read than tables of figures, but they can be misleading, especially when the scale shown in the vertical axis does not start at zero, or when the horizontal scale is compressed or extended. It is not unknown for this to be done deliberately when using two or more graphs to show rival products (see *Figure 7* on page 74).

When drawing graphs freehand it is sensible to use graph paper to ensure accuracy of scale. The ideal graph paper to use is the sort that is printed in a shade of grey that does not photocopy, so the end product is not filled with tiny shadowy squares. If grid lines are required, they can be drawn in with a fine pencil or pen.

Figure 6b: Table (2)

MONTHLY WIDGET PRODUCTION												
	J	F	M	A	M	J	J	A	S	O	N	D
No. of Machinists	23	23	22	21	21	21	22	20	23	23	23	22
Daily Widget Production	361	361	341	315	314	313	330	293	356	361	361	327
Average per Machinist	16	16	15.5	15	15	15	15	14.5	15.5	16	16	15

Bar charts

Bar charts, like graphs, are used to show trends or variations. They are used frequently in the investment business to show the difference in performance between investment products such as unit trusts and the humbler building society deposit. They are clearest when comparing

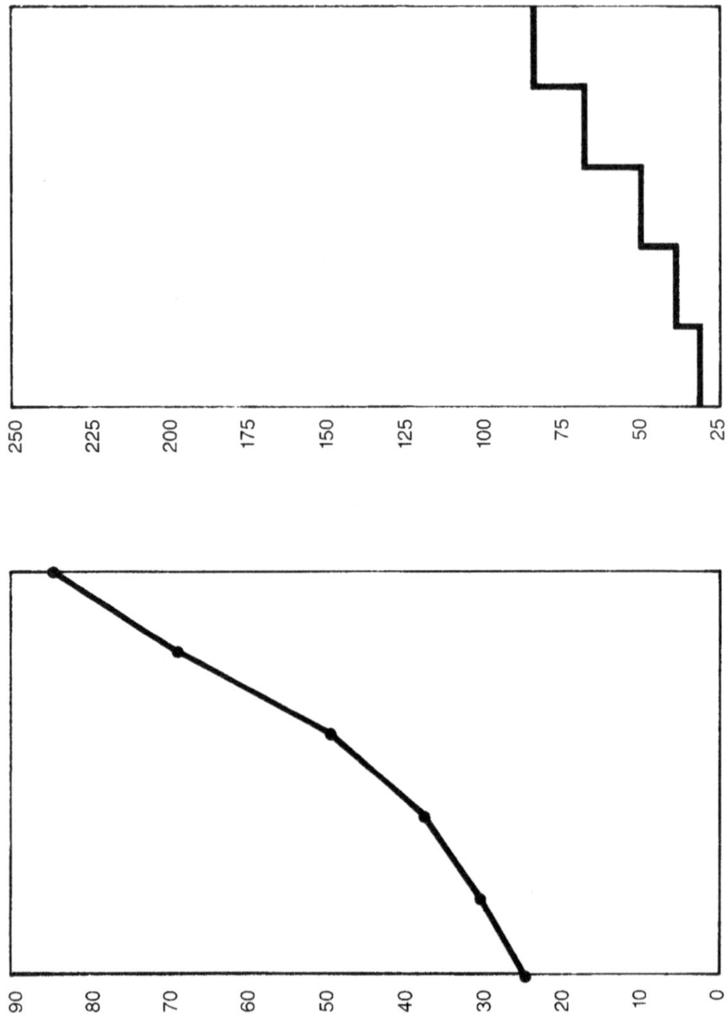

Figure 7: Rival Products

only two items, but can be used for more if the size of the chart and the scope for different shadings or colour printing permits. In general, the more items there are, the better it is to use a series of charts.

The width of the bars should not be varied in an attempt to show more than one aspect in each chart since this serves only to distort the picture. Where the intention is to show an expansion beyond both the trend and the scale of the chart, it is better to "break" the bar with a zigzag and add a figure to indicate the magnitude.

Pie charts

Pie charts are used to show proportions — literally as slices of a pie. They are popular in financial reports, often being used to show, for example, how a local council allocates its income between education, garbage collection and so on.

Newspapers sometimes present these in fanciful forms, such as mortgage figures shown as divisions of the top of a chimney pot complete with television aerial and tiled roof. This is not a good idea in business reports as it tends to trivialise rather than to enhance the data. For serious information it is best to stick to simple illustrations.

Pie charts should be drawn as accurately as possible and the actual value of each slice should be shown. Too many slices spoil the visual impact, so that if there are many more or less equal slices it is better to use a different type of diagram. Where there are a few big slices and many slices which are too small for the value of each to be shown easily, a "magnifying glass" technique can be used to pull out and enlarge the section containing the small slices (see *Figure 8* overleaf).

Pictograms

These are charts which use pictures instead of numbers. The pictures will be in the form of silhouettes or very simple stylised figures. They are popular with newspapers, which use them to show such things as troop movements, with rows of tanks, aeroplanes and battleships; and with insurance companies who use them to present accident statistics or mortality tables. Other uses might be to show gender and age split of a local population, types of pet kept by school children or methods of holiday transport.

Being rather simplistic, pictograms can easily appear patronising and are thus inappropriate for formal business reports. They should not be attempted by anyone other than a professional artist unless the items chosen are available as stencils, transfers or computer graphics (see *Figure 9* overleaf).

Figure 8: Pie Chart

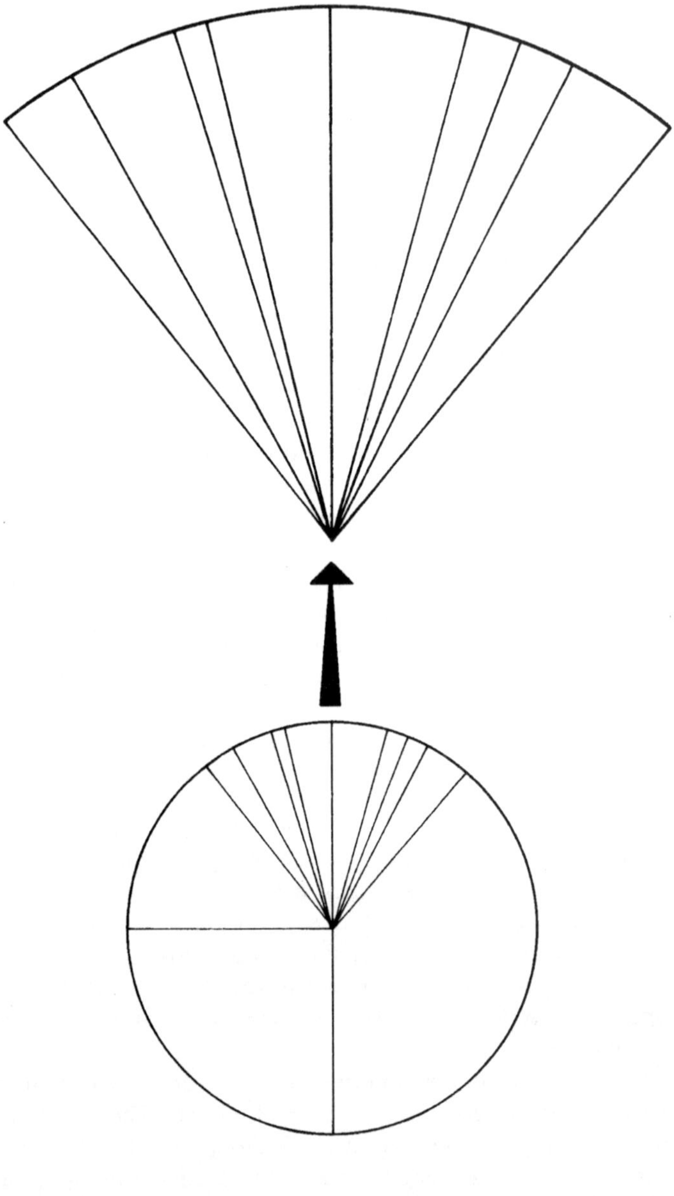

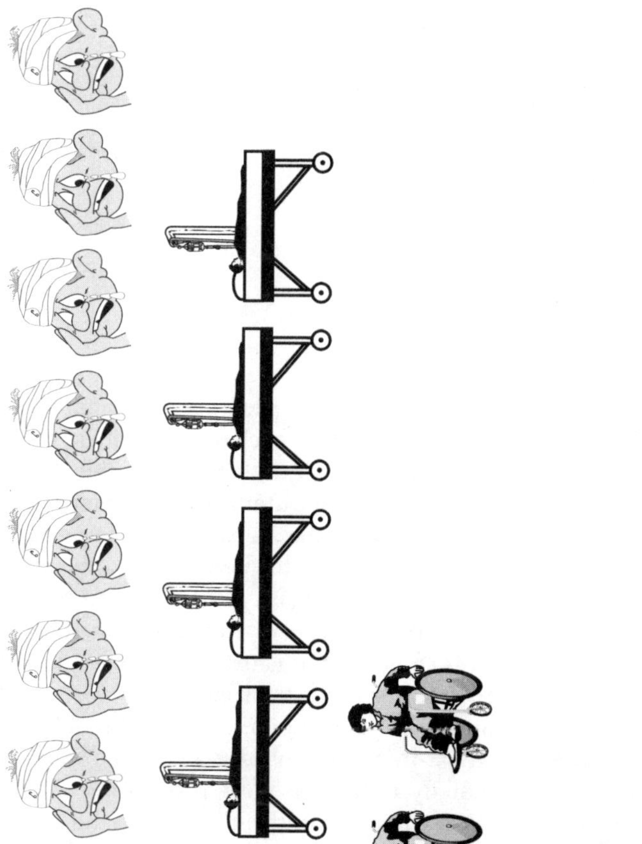

Figure 9: Pictogram

Other Information

Where the information to be conveyed is not numerical there are still conventions as to the form which should be used. Those most commonly seen are:

- flow charts
- genealogical tables
- maps and plans
- line drawings
- photographs.

Flow charts

These charts consist of a series of instructions or questions which are often shown inside boxes connected to each other by lines. The boxes are not strictly necessary, but do show at a glance what the chart is for.

Flow charts originated in the computer industry where they are still used by systems analysts to chart the steps needed to perform a task. There are conventions among computer people as to the shape of the box used to show different actions, eg a cylinder is used to indicate use of a disk drive, but for other purposes the shape of the box is less important as long as it is consistent. It is usual to insert questions into a different shape of box than for other instructions.

The basic principle in flow charting is that only the relevant factors are shown. They are most frequently used to show the steps needed to complete a task or to analyse the cause of a problem.

Instead of writing a sentence full of "if" clauses, the use of a flow chart involves just two options by posing a series of questions which can only be answered "yes" or "no". The skill in writing a good flow chart lies in phrasing each question so that all the "yes" answers flow in one line and all the "no" replies flow in another. This lessens the risk of mistakes being made by those who are following a chart.

Where a "yes" answer is essential to taking the correct step, "no" replies usually lead round a circuit of further instructions that go back to the starting point. These circles can end up as a confusing series of concentric circles if care is not taken in the drafting.

The only "rules" relating to flow chart construction are that the flow should be from top to bottom and left to right and that there should be no crossed lines (see *Figure 10* opposite).

Figure 10: Flow Chart

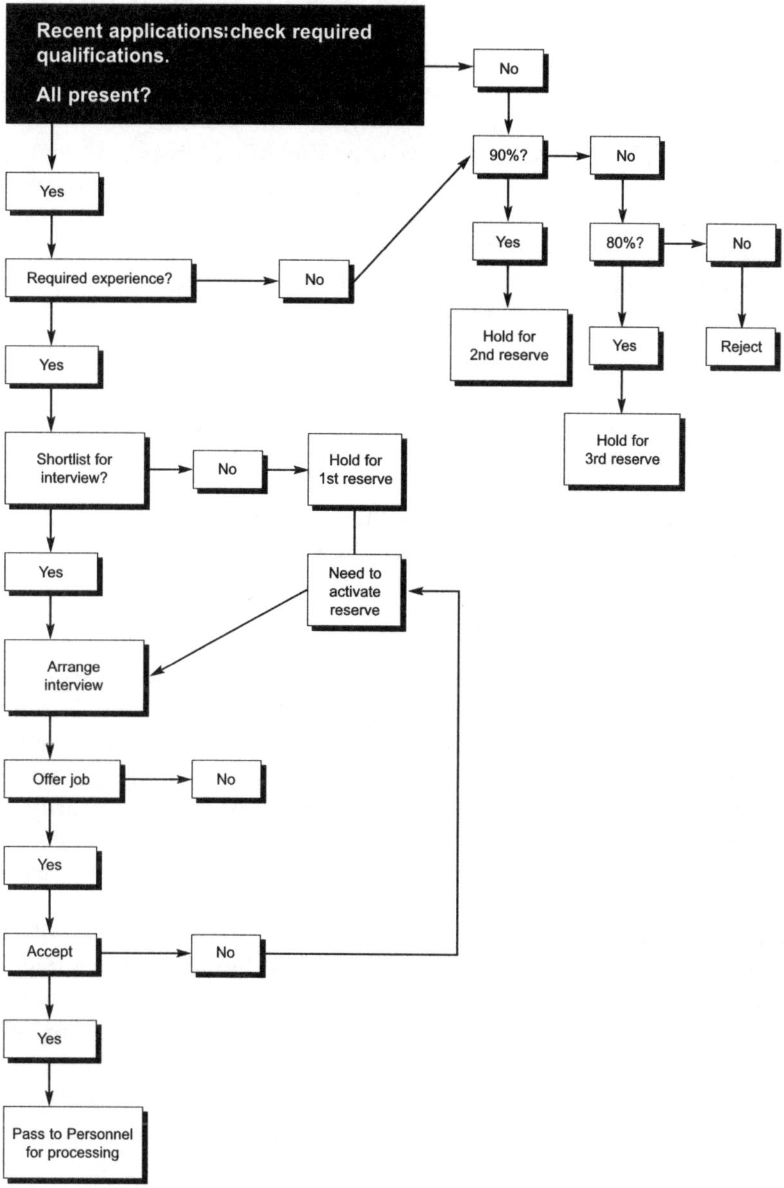

Genealogical tables

These are generally used to show management structures (see *Figure 11* opposite). They are usually drawn to show the most senior position at the top. Where the structure is complex, junior staff can be shown by a number or in a subsidiary table. Organisational convention dictates whether names of job holders are shown, or the job title.

Genealogical tables can also be used for other purposes, such as shareholding structures or the stages involved in building a complex product such as a car. In other words, anything which has a pyramid-like structure can be shown in this way.

These tables often need to be dated: where job structures or the names of individuals are shown, this is essential.

Maps and plans

These have already been discussed in *Chapter 3: Collecting and Organising Information* in connection with accident reports, but they are used for many other purposes, such as:

- locating sites of commercial or political significance
- indicating demographic details within a country
- showing destinations and routes of transport systems
- showing variations in terrain
- showing reorganisation of floor space.

North should always be shown on maps, even when it seems unnecessary to the writer and both maps and plans should include a statement of the scale, either as a small scale in a corner, or as a legend, eg "1cm =1km".

Depending on what they depict, maps need not necessarily be meticulously drawn so long as what they portray is obvious. The commonest candidates for impressionistic shapes are outlines of countries and continents.

Maps should not be cluttered with too much information. As with pie charts, it is better to use the magnifying glass technique to pull out areas of special interest.

It is common practice to photocopy maps and attach these to reports, but this practice is an infringement of copyright unless permission is granted. Another method is to trace a rough map from a published map and strictly speaking, this also infringes copyright. However, there are now many maps available on CD-ROM, or for downloading from the Internet and the conditions attached to using these will be found with the general instructions on reproducing them.

Figure 11: Genealogical Table

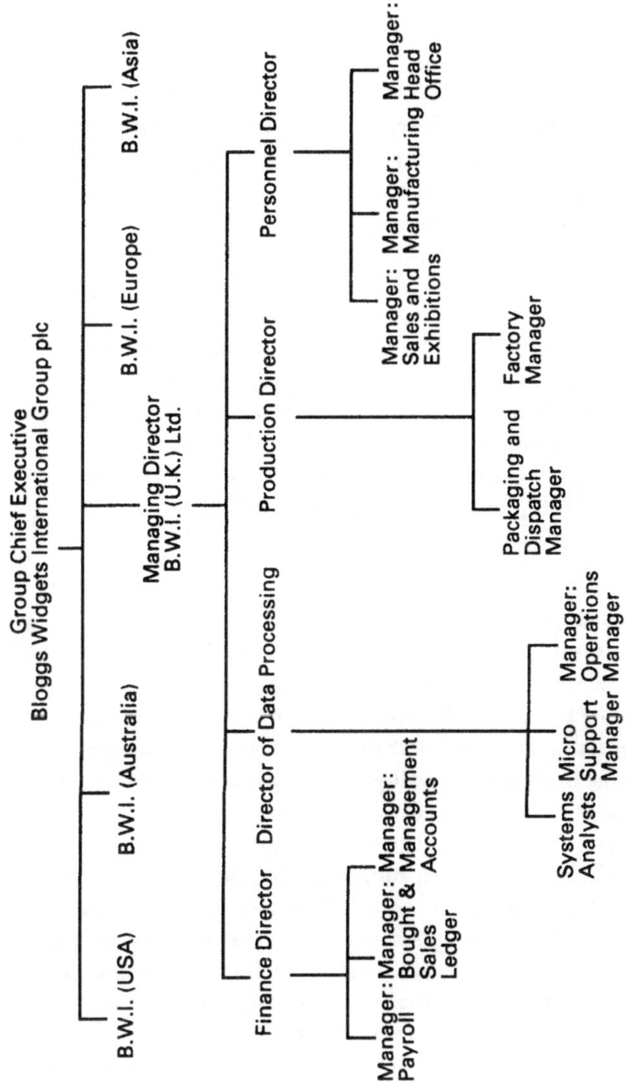

Line drawings

These are most commonly used to show the dimensions of a complex object such as an engine, or to show its component parts. Whatever their purpose, they must be correct and precise and for these reasons should only be drawn by professional technical artists.

Manufacturers may require "orthographic" drawings, which are scale plans of the four main views — top, sides, back and front; or "exploded" drawings of the components making up a complex product. These show each component pulled away from its companions so that each can be seen in the correct relationship, rather than as a set of drawings of each individual part.

"Isometric" drawings show the whole object without perspective, while "perspective" drawings give a layman a better idea of what the object looks like. Where items exist in reality rather than in a designer's imagination, a photograph may be preferred.

There are many computer programs which offer various levels of drawing facilities, but these do require a fair degree of expertise to produce good results. There is also plenty of "clip-art" available, but very little of it is suitable for use in reports.

Photographs

When the report writer wants only to show the readers what something looks like, photographs are probably easier to produce than line drawings. However where the intention is to make some point about the object or place involved, it is often better to use a line drawing which can show only that which is relevant and even exaggerate particular aspects to ensure the point is made.

Digital pictures or scanned photographs can be enhanced by skilled users of the relevant computer software, but unless the report writer has this expertise, it may cost as much or more to get it done than to engage an artist to produce line drawings. The quality of the end product usually bears a direct relationship to the cost of the equipment used, including that used for printing the end product.

In general, line drawings are better for report illustrations than photographs. This does not mean, however, that the artist has to go to the object since even the most amateur of photographers can produce a reasonable Polaroid picture or rough sketch for guidance.

As with maps, there are many images available on CD-ROM or on the Internet.

PRESENTING ILLUSTRATIONS

Useful though illustrations are, they should not be added to a report unless there is a good reason for their presence. As with other information, if it does not further the purpose of the report, it should be omitted, no matter how difficult it was to obtain and no matter how attractive it is. Extraneous illustrations only puzzle and distract the reader.

Location

No illustration is self-explanatory, so not only should it be referred to in the text, but it should be placed as close to the relevant portion of the text as possible, provided that this does not involve dissecting a paragraph. Ideally, the reader should be able to see the illustration while reading the text about it. It is extremely irritating to have to turn pages to find illustrations.

Titles

Even when they are placed immediately adjacent to the text in which they are discussed, all illustrations should be titled and numbered. The title should be placed at the head or foot of the illustration, not at the side where it could be interpreted as a label for part of the picture rather than a heading for the whole thing.

Numbering Illustrations

Numbers can be allocated in two ways, namely:
- sequentially through the report
- sequentially throughout each section, with the section number preceding the sequence number, thus: Fig.2.2.

The first method is easier to follow, but organisational convention may preclude its use.

Abbreviations

Abbreviations are a common cause of confusion in reports. This confusion can be avoided by using British Standards unless organisational convention differs. These differing conventions are most likely to be encountered in multinational companies and it is sensible in such cases to include a section on abbreviations in the glossary. One abbreviation that often causes confusion is the presentation of dates. In

Britain, "10/12/03" means 10 December 2003. In America it means 12 October. For this reason, columns showing dates should be headed "DD/MM/YY" or "MM/DD/YY" as appropriate. In other situations the month should be written in words. A three letter abbreviation of the month is acceptable in tables or graphs but not in the text of the formal report. In these, the month and year should be shown in full.

Care should be taken with single letter abbreviations, as upper and lower case may mean different things. The lower-case letter "m" means "metre", but "M" means "million". There is no need to pluralise abbreviations by adding an "s" at the end. For example, "m" means "metres" as well as "metre". Full stops should not be added to abbreviations unless they occur at the end of a sentence.

Layout

Illustrations should be set within the same margins as the text. This does not mean that they must not be smaller, only that they should not overflow, since this gives the impression that something went wrong with the printing.

Margins serve to create a frame round both the text and illustrations which allow the eye to accept the information easily. Empty spaces within illustrations serve the same purpose and when they occur naturally in a graph or other diagram, they should be left empty instead of being cluttered up with explanatory words.

Where an illustration occupies a whole page, it may be easier on the eye when presented in landscape format (longer than high) instead of portrait format (higher than long). In this case the bottom of the picture should be on the right, so that the turn is clockwise, in the same way as the column headings.

Physical Production

When the report writer has to prepare the diagrams by hand without the assistance of an artist, the main thing to consider is clarity. A fine-nibbed drafting pen should always be used. These pens are designed to draw lines at a constant thickness. Nibs of 0.5mm will suit most diagrams.

Unless the report is to be printed or photocopied in colour, black ink should always be used. When the report is to be photocopied it is worth using the grey-printed graph paper which does not photocopy, to give accurate lines and right angles.

Compasses and a protractor should always be used to draw circles and measure angles accurately. Many other shapes are available as stencils from graphic art supply shops.

COPYRIGHT

The report writer is responsible for obtaining any necessary permission to use copyright materials. As well as illustrations from CD-ROMs or the Internet, this includes anything copied from books or other published documents and may even include photographs taken especially for the report, unless the contract with the photographer specifies otherwise.

Permission to use copyright material is not given in a blanket form, but is valid only for a single specified purpose, unless otherwise stated.

SUMMARY

Words are not always the ideal way to convey information. The use of illustrations can save space and they have more impact than many lines of prose. Illustrations fall naturally into two types: those used for numerical data and those used for other purposes. In each case, a particular type of illustration is chosen according to convention.

There are many computer programs which offer drawing facilities, but these do require some expertise to obtain good results. Some maps, photographs or other illustrative material are available on CD-ROM or on the Internet.

All illustration should relate to matters discussed in the text and should be ideally located close to that text. They should be numbered and titled and any abbreviations used in the captions or column headings should be based on British Standards or local conventions.

It is the report writer's responsibility to obtain permission to use copyright material.

CHAPTER 8

PRODUCTION AND DISTRIBUTION

After all the preliminary stages of writing are completed, some thought should be given to preparing the manuscript for typing. Whether this is done by the writer or someone else, even the most experienced secretary will need to be told how the report should be presented.

Good layout is essential if the report is to have the desired impact on its readers. It would be a pity if it receives a lukewarm reception because its physical appearance is mediocre.

PRESENTATION

Unless there is a standard format within the organisation, a set of instructions should be compiled on a separate sheet. This should specify:

- presentation of titles and headings
- spacing and margins
- symbols to be used
- justification of lines and paragraphs
- typeface
- page numbering.

Titles and Headings

The title should stand out, either by using a different typeface, block capitals, bold type or underlining. It should be centred in its own space on the page, with nothing to distract the reader's eye. Unless the report is an informal one in memo form, there should be a separate title page.

As this is the first thing the reader sees, this should create a good impression and to avoid a cluttered look it should contain no more than four items:

- the title and the fact that it is a report
- the name of the writer or writers
- if it is not the final version, the number of the draft
- the date of issue.

Within the report, section headings should also stand out, but not quite as strongly as the main title. Each level of section heading and sub-section heading should reduce by one degree of magnitude, so if the main title is in bold block capitals underlined, section headings should omit either the underlining or the emboldening. Subheadings should omit the other, or could be in lower-case underlined or bold.

Spacing and Margins

In short informal reports there should be double line spacing between sections. This makes it clear to readers that they have reached the end of the section and it should also be remembered that short blocks of text are inviting to read whereas long, unbroken sections are daunting.

In longer formal reports, each main section should start on a new page; for complex reports this may also be desirable for some sub-sections.

Margins should be reasonably wide without leaving so much space that the text looks cramped in the middle of the page. The type of binding to be used should be considered when setting the margins.

Symbols

Where symbols are used, they should not only be consistent throughout, but should, wherever possible, be those which are generally accepted:

1. Dots are used to indicate parts omitted from quotations, with three dots meaning less than a sentence and six dots meaning at least a whole sentence.
2. Where the writer has had to insert an explanation into a quotation, for instance to explain who "he" is, this insertion should be in square brackets, thus: [ ]. This is particularly important where figures are concerned, as ordinary brackets signify a deficit.

3. Where there is some doubt as to the truth of a quoted statement, or where there is an apparent mis-spelling, the word "sic", which means "as it is written" should be added in brackets immediately after the dubious item.

Some writers use italics for quotations. This is only acceptable for brief quotations and where there are few of them. Excessive use of italics is distracting to the eye and gives a restless feel to the text.

Justification

This should clarify whether all type should be left "ragged" or justified to the right margin and whether paragraphs should be indented or blocked. The modern tendency is for paragraphs to be blocked and separated by a line space.

Typeface or Font

In the rare situation where there is not a standard within the organisation, it is best to choose a conservative font such as Times New Roman. Fancy fonts such as Gothic or Script are almost never appropriate. If writing a report for an outside organisation, a decision will have to be made on which organisation's preferred font to use.

Page Numbering

The pages of any document more that two pages long should be numbered. To a certain extent the location of the numbers is a matter of personal choice or organisational convention. However, where the report is to be bound or printed on both sides of the paper, there are some special considerations: if it is to be bound and single sided, numbers in left hand corners are inadvisable as they will be difficult to see. If it is to be double sided, neither corner is advisable as the numbering will have to be delayed until the final version and then put on alternate left and right corners.

To avoid such problems, the best place is the centre of the page, preferably at the top as this allows easy reference when looking for a specific page.

Pages should be numbered as soon as they are typed, to avoid losing the sequence if they are dropped. For this reason, manuscript pages should also be numbered. The location of separate illustrations must be clearly indicated, as they will have to be included in the numbering sequence.

The title page should not be numbered. The contents list is not usually numbered. The summary is best numbered in roman numerals as it may be removed from the report to take on a life of its own.

CHECKING

Regardless of who typed the report, the writer must check it carefully before launching it onto the outside world.

Two types of check should be carried out and the longer the report, the more sensible it is to do these checks as separate operations.

The first is a physical proofread, which should not be relegated to a computerised spell-check. It is surprising how often simple keying errors serve to reverse the sense of important statements by the omission or alteration of one letter: "There is now concern ..." could become "There is no concern ...". Unfortunately, both are real words and word processor spell-checking programs will ignore them. This proves that spell-chequers are knot infallible! When accuracy is essential, nothing beats the human eye.

Long sequences of figures, if not produced on a spreadsheet should ideally be checked by two people, one reading from the manuscript while the other checks the print. If assistance is not available, each set of figures should be totalled on a calculator, first on the manuscript, then on the print. If the two totals agree, there is no need to check the accuracy of the figures, but the eye should still be run down each column in case any of the figures is out of alignment.

The second check is for sense and logic. If the deadline allows, at least two days should elapse between completing the writing process and checking the printed version. This allows the writer to forget the actual words used and thus to look properly at it instead of assuming that each phrase is reproduced as it was written. For this reason, although the writer should do the first check, a third party should also check it for incongruities the writer may have missed. Another reason for using a third party is that the writer often gets carried away by the brilliance of the writing and just reads on through the script instead of actually checking it.

Everything must be checked. Errors are just as likely to occur in the title page, contents list or diagram captions as in the main text. Particular care must be taken to check names. Irritation at the least and mortal offence at worst can be caused by carelessness over people's names and companies' titles.

Such carelessness casts doubt on the value of the rest of the report. The inference is always that it is the writer who is sloppy or ignorant and thus unprofessional, rather than the typist.

REPRODUCTION

When using outside printers or distant in-house reprographics departments, unless the style of printing is a matter of organisational convention or the writer is sufficiently expert to give precise instructions, all aspects should be discussed with the printer. These discussions should, as well as the aspects discussed above, cover binding, paper quality, finish and colour.

Binding

Although binding is the last in the sequence of processes, the choice of binding must come first, because of its effect on page layout and print sequencing.

Ideally, all reports should open to lie flat. It is annoying to have to hold down the pages of a book or a document when its binding will not allow it to open up completely without disintegrating. However, the practicalities of most report production are that they are printed or photocopied and bound in-house. In this situation, the binding tends to be of a type that captures a portion of the edge of the paper. Margins must be wide enough to allow for this, or text and figures disappear into the binding. Binding methods include the following.

1. Full book-type binding, with sewn pages and hard covers, or "perfect" binding, where the back edges of the pages are trimmed and glued before a soft cover is added. This method is less robust and may not be suitable for more than 100 pages or for glossy paper.
2. Booklet binding with sewn or stapled centres (known as saddle-stitching).
3. Spiral or ring bindings. Although bulky, these are probably the most satisfactory for large reports as they look reasonably professional and allow the pages to open flat.
4. Plastic combs. This is a cheaper process which allows the pages to open flat. The combs are available in various colours and can themselves carry simple printed titles.
5. Slide binders. These are cheaper still, but do not allow the pages to open flat. They will take up to 25 pages.

6. Staples. These are very cheap but only suitable for internal reports. They allow the corners to fray and crease and even deep staples will not hold more than 25 pages.
7. Treasury tags. Also very cheap but have an old fashioned image. If loose enough to permit the pages to open flat they soon tear away from the holes.
8. Paper clips are acceptable for very short informal reports.
9. Pins will only hold three or four pages, are a nuisance to handle and tend to draw blood, so are not a good idea.

Wherever possible, bound reports should have a cover, even if it is no more than a sheet of clear plastic.

Text Colour

Nothing is as easy to read as black print on white paper. Blues and greys are unnecessarily fanciful and can be very difficult to read in poor light or when printed on tinted paper. Red or green should be avoided, as these are the two colours which cannot be distinguished by the colour-blind, who see both as grey. This is a very common condition and thus should not be overlooked.

All text should be printed in the same colour, the only exception being captions for illustrations in some types of informal report.

Choice of Paper

White paper is the cheapest and, for most purposes, the best choice. If colours are to be used, they should not be so dark that it is difficult to read the printing.

Long and complex reports can benefit from different colours for different sections, but there should be a discernible logic in the choice of colours. If appendices are specific to certain sections, they should be in the same colour as the sections to which they relate. A cheaper alternative to different colours for each section is to separate the sections with one blank sheet of coloured paper.

The quality and finish of the paper is important, not only to the perceived value and impact of the report, but also to its physical longevity. Good matt-finish bond paper is the most commonly used for all purposes and thus the cheapest. The actual thickness or "weight" is usually a matter of organisational choice, but the general principle is to use the best that the budget allows. Gloss-finish or art paper is more expensive, not only because of the processes involved in its manufacture but also because it is less commonly used than matt-finish. It is not always easy to read, especially in artificial light and some types of binding glue do not stick to it properly. However, gloss-paper is generally more robust and resistant to soiling than matt varieties.

Photocopying

Reproduction by photocopying is an acceptable method for internal reports.

The average office photocopier, assuming that it is properly maintained, will give good copies of black type and diagrams on various colours of paper. Ordinary black and white copiers will produce murky results from coloured diagrams, so thought must be given to differentiation of shading in graphs and charts.

Organisations with reprographic departments or commercial print shops will have more sophisticated machines and it is worth consulting the machine operator to find out what facilities are available.

EARLY DRAFTS

A high proportion of reports, especially those which are complex, need to go through several drafts before the final version can be signed off and distributed. The early drafts have to be circulated to various interested parties for comments and suggestions which then have to be incorporated into the final version.

Example: Report on a Scheme for Staff Working at Home

Draft One offered two options, of full-time work at home or a set number of days per week, and was circulated to:

- the information technology director for comments on provision of computer hardware and software
- the legal department for comments on how the scheme would affect employment contracts and also on insurance implications
- the personnel department who would have to provide staff to monitor the scheme
- the company's tax expert for comments on tax and business use rating implications for the company and the recipients
- heads of departments whose staff are most likely to work under the schemes.

Draft Two incorporated the comments and suggestions of all the above and offered some tentative recommendations on how to deal with various aspects. It was circulated to all the parties listed above and the company's insurers for their further comments.

Draft Three was considerably refined and included some specific recommendations. It was circulated to all members of the executive committee for discussion and decision at a board meeting.

Draft Four was the final version, giving full details of the agreed scheme. It was circulated to all the parties listed above and the entire staff, finally being incorporated in the documentation to be given to all new staff.

The Draft Process

The draft process takes time and requires tactful control. The more people who are involved, the greater the necessity for documentary control mechanisms, whether on paper or by electronic methods. Some decisions which have to be made early on are:

- whether to send the whole of each draft to everyone, or only to send each recipient the portions relevant to their areas
- whether recipients will be allowed to make copies
- whether persons not on the original distribution list should be allowed to see copies — if they are, it is better for them to receive a numbered copy from the distribution controller than to be allowed to make their own copy of someone else's
- whether to require copies of early drafts to be returned to the controller — this may be desirable not only where the content is highly controversial or confidential, but also to avoid confusion between early and later drafts
- how to number drafts — as a general principle, each page of each draft should not only be numbered, but carry the fact that it is a draft and which version.

HARD COPIES

With a very large circulation list a pro-forma sheet should be devised. This will call for a list of all the recipients of each draft, with dates of dispatch, return deadlines and actual return. A safety factor of several days should be built in to return dates.

As each copy of each draft, or the comments on it, comes back, it should be checked to be sure it is complete and a note made of which section(s) need following up or rewriting.

Each person on the circulation list should receive their own copy. This avoids delays and the risk of the reports being broken up by people taking out sections that interest them before passing the rest on.

Ideally, each copy should be numbered and show how many copies are in circulation, eg "6 of 24". In some organisations it may be necessary to exercise tact when allocating numbered copies to different levels of management. Circulation lists in alphabetical order and allocation of numbers from top down should eliminate any nonsense about seniority.

ELECTRONIC CIRCULATION

The only differences in this method to that of circulating paper copies are:

- where the contents are confidential, rather than actually sending the draft to recipients, it should be made available, by password only, from a secure file
- ideally, where confidential or not, drafts should be available in Read Only format so no unauthorised alterations creep in
- where large amounts of information is in illustrative form (eg graphs, etc), some thought should be given to whether people accessing this from remote locations on portable computers have enough capacity to download them in a reasonable time.

LATER DRAFTS

Any alterations to the original version mean that the entire report will have to be revised again to check for contradiction, illogicality, consistency and balance. Only the portions that have been altered need proofreading.

It is particularly important to check for changes of style if large passages contributed by other persons have to be inserted. It may be preferable to put these in the appendices, or at the end of the section over the contributor's signature. Where the contributor holds high rank, it may be preferable to both parties to insert the contribution as a foreword, especially if it is made on the premise "I'm in charge, so I must make my mark".

THE ACCOMPANYING MEMO

Depending on the degree of formality in the organisation, this may not need to say more than "Here is the first draft of the report I mentioned to you on the telephone. Please let me have it back with your comments, by the 7th".

Where outsiders are concerned, this memo (or letter) may need to explain why the recipient has been chosen, which sections are involved and the nature of the desired contribution. It will also have to cover the nature of the acknowledgements and may need to enquire about a fee.

PRESENTATION TO BUSINESS MEETINGS

While all reports should stand on their own, some individuals and organisations like to have a personal presentation with an opportunity for questions and discussion.

There is little difference between presenting a report and any other sort of business presentation, except that copies of the report should be circulated in advance. The writer should read through the report as many times as necessary to ensure complete familiarity before making the presentation. If there are any areas where additional expertise may be needed for expansion or questions, those experts should be organised and briefed.

All the illustrations should be put onto slides or whatever medium is necessary for the available projection equipment. For less formal presentations where a flip-chart may be used, this should be prepared, either completely or in the form of reference points which make it easy to draw freehand at the appropriate time in the presentation.

There are various computer programs such as Microsoft Powerpoint which can be used for presentations. A little practice is advisable before attempting to create an important presentation this way. The temptation to use too many colours or other features of such programs should be resisted, as this tends to confuse more than it enhances.

SUMMARY

Presentation and layout are important if the impact of a report is not to be diminished. Consistency in reprographic style is also important, as is careful proofreading. Computer spell-checkers should not be trusted to do an adequate job. Page numbering, margins, type of binding and colour of print and paper all have their part to play in the look of a report and should be carefully considered.

Many reports have to be circulated in draft form, either in paper or electronic form, for comments before the final version is prepared. These drafts should be identified by issue number and their circulation should be controlled. A date for comments should be set.

Some reports have to be presented at meetings, where the presenter will need visual aids and must expect to receive questions.

CHAPTER 9

SAMPLE REPORTS

SAMPLE REPORT 1: A SHORT SIMPLE REPORT

Memo

To: Ms Boss
From: Ms Assistant
Date: 31 May 2001
Subject: Staff holidays

As you requested, I have looked into the matter of staff coverage during the peak holiday months of July and August.
With the exception of the Bought Ledger section, there are no sections where more than one person will be away simultaneously and those sections will cover the necessary work by use of the flexi-time system.
Bought Ledger will have three people away during the last two weeks in August. This is unavoidable as in each case there are school children and the spouse has no option of alternative holiday dates.
Despite the willingness of the other staff in this section to work overtime, there could still be a problem as the month-end approaches. We may need to think of getting in at least one temp to ease the burden.

SAMPLE REPORT 2: A BRIEF INFORMAL REPORT

Mobile phones

A report by Kathleen O'Donoghue
On the need to rationalise mobile phone use within the company

28 March 2001

Circulation:
F Bloggs
C Brown

H Higgins

Introduction

The situation has arisen where company employees have arranged for, and are using, a variety of mobile phones and mobile phone networks, charging the company for their use through expense accounts. This is proving complex to administer and may not be the most economic way to maintain contact with essential employees when they are out of the office.
The purpose of this report is to investigate the available networks, handsets and charge bands, with a view to rationalising and monitoring mobile phone usage and to obtain the best service and most economic rates.

Summary

1. The current situation is costing the company some £1800 per month in expenses claimed by 41 employees. It is estimated that 27 other employees would like to have mobile phones, which would bring this cost up to about £3000 per month.
2. It currently takes two man-days to check expense claims. This would increase to four if the number of users rose to 70.
3. The company's current costs do not include anything for purchasing or insuring handsets.
4. There are currently no problems in maintaining contact with users. The majority seem happy to continue as they are doing.
5. If the company takes over provision of mobile phone handsets and service, there will be an initial cost of £3500 and annual insurance costs of £2000. Extra handsets will have to be held to cope with malfunctioning and stolen handsets.
6. Staff time expenditure will increase by 50% if the company provides handsets and contracts with a service provider.

Conclusions and recommendations

We currently have a system which works adequately and costs less in both expenses paid and staff time than it would if we were to provide mobile phones direct.

I therefore recommend that we do nothing to alter this situation immediately, but investigate and report annually, as the number of employees wishing to have mobile phones may increase to the point where it would be more economic for the company to provide them.

Investigation into the current situation

1. Some 41 employees currently charge the company for business mobile phone use, using six different service suppliers and with an average monthly cost of £1763. Eighteen of these are senior managers (or more senior) and spend much of their time on the road. They account for about two-thirds of this cost. A further 27 employees have enquired about obtaining mobile phones, of whom some 12 spend much of their time outside the office. On the same level of charge costs, this would bring the monthly cost to about £3000.
2. It currently occupies a little more two man-days per month to check these expense claims and account for VAT. It would take four man-days if the additional 27 employees used the same method of reclaiming their costs.
3. The company currently makes no contribution towards the cost of purchasing or insuring handsets, nor does it get involved in managing the telephones.
4. There are currently rarely any problems in making contact with users through their mobile phones. A few would prefer the company to provide their phones, but the majority seem happy to continue as they are doing.
5. To provide handsets and service for 70 people will cost an initial outlay of £3500. Handset insurance will cost approximately £2000 annually. The two main service providers, Cellfone and Vodonet, are both keen to obtain a contract with us. Costs and available facilities are more or less the same.
6. Staff time checking service invoices will increase as the whole of each invoice will have to be checked for personal calls. This extra time is estimated to bring the total time expended to six man-days per month.

- A list of individuals currently using mobile telephones and their average monthly call costs is attached.
- Copies of bids from Cellfone and Vodonet to provide handsets and service are attached.

SAMPLE REPORT 3: A FORMAL REPORT

e-commerce

A report on long-term strategic implications of the new electronic marketplace
by Kathleen O'Donoghue

21 March 2001

Contents

Introduction

In order to maintain its position as a market leader, Bloggins Widgets plc cannot ignore the new opportunities which have opened up through the Internet. It was believed that many customers would prefer to order direct through a website instead of the current system of post, telephone and visits from representatives.

The company needs to acquire the necessary hardware and expertise to offer such a service to its customers.

This report follows an investigation into:

- customer preferences and requirements
- computer hardware and staffing requirements
- suitable locations for a new e-commerce department
- methods of delivery of products
- potential difficulties inherent in engaging in e-commerce
- timescale and costs.

Executive summary

Customer preferences and requirements

A survey carried out among representative numbers of wholesale and retail customer showed that over 75% of both would prefer to use a computerised ordering system. Wholesale customers would not be prepared to sacrifice their current payment terms. Retail customers would be happy to pay immediately by credit card.

Computer hardware and staffing requirements

In order to provide the necessary service, a powerful computer is required. The ideal is the new Krey Sooperdooper Mark 3. To produce and test the software programs, a team of 12 analysts and programmers will be required for six months. After this, a maintenance team of four people will be required. As an alternative to buying our own hardware and employing our own software teams, we might consider contracting either or both aspects to an outside organisation.

Suitable locations for a new e-commerce department

Confidentiality and space requirements for a team of 12 people requires a location outside Head Office for the development stages. Space for four people after that can be made available at Head Office. While there is no particular reason for these staff to be located there, such people are in high demand and reluctant to work at any great distance from central London. Computer security requires that the machine be located away from Head Office and a suitable site will have to be found.

Methods of delivery of products

There are three possible methods of delivery products:

1. Using our current wholesaler, or changing to another wholesaler.
2. Setting up our own warehouse and despatch facility.
3. Using a mail order 'fulfilment house'.

Potential difficulties inherent in engaging in e-commerce

As with any new venture, there are potential problems with e-commerce. These include payment security, which is a primary concern of customers, reliability of computer hardware and software and delivery delays. This latter is not a problem associated specially with e-commerce, unless triggered by failures in the system which do not pass orders to the delivery facility in a timely fashion.

Timescale and costs

To create our own software and receive our own hardware, test and get our own system up and running smoothly will take 18 to 24 months. This will cost £5 million. Ongoing costs will be close to £1 million per year. To utilise the services of an outside computer service company experienced in e-commerce to have a system up and running will take six to nine months. This will have an initial cost of £2.5 million, plus, if desired, ongoing costs of between £1.5 million and £2 million per year, dependent on the length of the contract. It will be necessary to consult our bankers on the best way to finance these costs.

Conclusions

In view of the enthusiasm of our customers for this method of ordering, and the dangers of losing market share to our competitors who are rumoured to be considering these methods, we should enter this new market place as soon as possible.

Recommendations

In order to avoid any loss of time, we should adopt a two-part strategy:

1. Start by using an outside service company, with their minimum contract period of two years.
2. At the same time, we should purchase our own new computer and create a new department to run our own system. This should include using a joint approach for delivery of a wholesaler for trade customers and a mail-order fulfilment house for retail customers.

This will require setting up a project team immediately to:

- find a suitable service company and negotiate the best possible terms for a two year contract
- discuss funding methods with the bank and our stock brokers
- order appropriate computer hardware and oversee its installation and testing
- recruit and brief suitable staff, including a department head
- design and write the necessary software
- find a suitable wholesaler and a suitable mail order fulfilment house and negotiate the best possible terms for contracts
- design a scheme for monitoring the success of this marketing method.

INDEX

G

H

I

Q

R

S